Praise for *Your Child is Not Broken*

"Everything we don't get but really want from a parenting class/coffee morning is in this book. It is neuro-affirmative, it is friendly, it is accessible and most importantly it is honestly imperfect and funny.

Full of great bits to pull out and share with family, friends and professionals in those moments we are so often lost for words.

Finally we have a book that will give every family the validation they are looking for."

Eliza Fricker, Missing The Mark blog

and *Sunday Times* Bestselling author

of *Can't Not Won't*

"Our education system is failing many of our children. When things go wrong at school, we too often decide the problem is the child and their family. Heidi's book vividly recounts her experience of being a parent to a child who couldn't thrive at school. We follow their journey from burnout to acceptance as they find a way to live and learn which works for them. It's a no-holds-barred, easy-to-read rollicking real-life story, and it shines a light onto an experience which is often invisible until you're living it."

– Dr. Naomi Fisher, Clinical Psychologist and author of *Changing Our Minds: How Children Can Take Control of their Own Learning*

"I highly recommend reading or listening to Heidi Mavir's book. Especially every parent who is struggling with their child in education and is feeling lost and alone. Her refreshing, open and honest tone brings home the importance of trusting your gut and being an advocate for your child. Her story highlights the issues many of us face in the education system and how trapped you can feel by well-meaning professionals. An absolute must-read!"

– Dr. Olivia Kessel, Clinician and Founder
of the SEND Parenting Podcast

"I've decided this book may as well just stay next to my laptop since I am either recommending it to pretty much every parent I speak to and every webinar I run and keep jumping up to grab it from my bookshelf!"

– Laura Kerbey, Cofounder and Director, Kite
Therapeutic Learning Service

Your Child Is Not Broken

Your Child Is Not Broken

Parent Your Neurodivergent Child Without Losing Your Marbles

Heidi Mavir

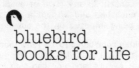

bluebird
books for life

First published 2022 by Authors & Co

This edition first published 2023 by Bluebird
an imprint of Pan Macmillan
The Smithson, 6 Briset Street, London EC1M 5NR
EU representative: Macmillan Publishers Ireland Ltd, 1st Floor,
The Liffey Trust Centre, 117–126 Sheriff Street Upper,
Dublin 1, D01 YC43
Associated companies throughout the world
www.panmacmillan.com

ISBN 978-1-0350-3057-6

5 7 9 8 6 4

A CIP catalogue record for this book is available from the British Library.

This book interior has been printed in Dyslexic font, designed to support
Neurodivergent readers.

Typeset in OpenDyslexic by Palimpsest Book Production Limited,
Falkirk, Stirlingshire

Printed and bound by CPI Group (UK) Ltd, Croydon, CR0 4YY

MIX
Paper | Supporting
responsible forestry
FSC® C116313

For Theo – you're my favourite.

Contents

Photograph © Nelly Naylor

About the Author

Heidi Mavir is a late-identified Neurodivergent adult. She is a public speaker, advocate, author, podcaster and parent to an Autistic/ADHD teenager. She is also a chronic oversharer and a bit of a badass.

In 2018 Heidi's son, Theo, experienced a mental health crisis, brought on by the struggles he faced in mainstream education as an undiagnosed Autistic student. Suddenly, Heidi found herself up the proverbial creek without any paddles. With Theo too unwell to attend school, or even leave the house, Heidi committed herself to finding out everything she could about neurodivergence; education, health and social care plans; and what it means to advocate for your disabled child in crisis.

Heidi took Theo's case to a SEN Tribunal and secured a bespoke package of education for him so that he had the support he needed to finish his GCSEs. As an extra surprise, during the process, Heidi also discovered that she is also Neurodivergent – at 44 years old!

Heidi has spoken openly about the impact the process had on her, sharing her experiences as a parent whose own mental health spiralled as a result of the overwhelming stress and pressure felt by parents of children unable to attend school.

A trained Mental Health First Aider and CPD Accredited Trauma-Informed Professional,

Heidi uses her knowledge, learning, and experience to help other parents and carers to become powerful advocates for their Neurodivergent kids. She has built an online community of over 6,000 families, supported by parent professionals and SEN advocates, who want to improve opportunities for Autistic learners. Heidi has spoken on stages across the UK. She has been featured in *The Sunday Times*, *The Guardian*, and on the BBC.

Heidi loves giraffes and will delight you with "giraf-facts", given the opportunity. Her guilty pleasures are posh gin, Yorkshire Tea, and her leopard print sofa, which cost more than her car. Heidi wishes all dresses had pockets.

You can find out more about Heidi, her work, and how to reach her at www.heidimavir.com

Foreword

Back in 2019, I recall being alerted to someone on social media sharing an image of themselves engaged in one of my online programmes, created specifically for parents to learn from an Autistic perspective about what autism actually is.

I saw the image of a woman sitting at a desk, watching me speak over a laptop, and I noticed instantly that she had guts. I started reading some of her content and watching her speak in small video clips and I learned more and more about just how determined she was.

That woman was Heidi.

Within a few weeks, we were chatting in an online meeting, where Heidi shared some really important information with me that – when taken into consideration when it comes to Autistic adults – was crucial as a collection of smaller pieces of a large picture called autism.

Lifelong mental health challenges, burnout and lingering fatigue, a child that could not attend school and was not supported in doing so by the very same institution they wanted to belong to. There were many other topics we discussed, and I don't remember the entire conversation; but I know it was enough for me to recognise that Heidi was, and is, Autistic.

When an Autistic person says that we recognise another as Autistic, it isn't disorder that we see. It's a kinship. I hear the same language of heart, the stories of generational trauma, the outpouring of sadness of an experience of parenthood disconnected and completely disempowered by oppressive systems that operate within the bounds of shame and parental blame and gaslighting.

When I recognise an Autistic person, I recognise strength. I identify someone who has continued on, against all odds. I see and hear, I sense gentleness coupled with a no-bullshit approach to life.

I know I've found neurokindred.

The incredible amount of families that I have had the privilege and honour of being in community with have demonstrated that there are stories; many stories of generational trauma, of bloodlines having

xx

gone unidentified, contributing to other forms of existential terror such as addiction, eating disorders, family violence, and many other outcomes of our ancestors not knowing who they are.

We are alive during a time when there is incredible opportunity and momentum for our voices to be heard. And yet, here we are, shielding our children from the trauma that a basic education can result in.

I am in awe of those parents that I meet with often, who realise their own neuro-divergence and move forward, carrying the torch of positive Autistic identity and culture.

As Autistic parents, we carry this message forth to help others discern between what has been termed as bad parenting, dysfunctional family life, and other ableist views, and the reality of our culture being different.

Different. Not dysfunctional.

A different way.

Of being, doing, living.

We seek to normalise our existence. Not disorders, not superheroes, just Autistic people.

This work we do is in order to save lives.

Thank you, Heidi, for carrying the torch.

Kristy Forbes, autism and neurodiversity specialist and Founding Director of InTune Pathways

Preface

I'm glad you're here.

No, really. You are so welcome here.

I say that because – as the parent of a child who does life differently – I know what it's like to feel unwelcome. Being a parent of a neurodivergent child (or children) can be incredibly isolating. That's why I wrote this book: so that other parents might see they are not alone.

I also wrote this book because I feel like it's time we get really bloody honest about the level of bullshit and fuckery we face as parents of neurodivergent kids. So, you'll find here some no-nonsense, sometimes-sweary accounts of some of my experiences as a parent of a late-identified Autistic child. Warts and all. With rants aplenty and hopefully the occasional nugget of wisdom too.

Back in 2019, in the first few months of my getting to grips with the idea that my gloriously quirky but incredibly anxious teenager was an Autistic-as-Fuck-ADHD-er, I felt so alone. I was so confused. How could he be Autistic? He didn't look Autistic. My son, Theo, was articulate and outgoing and made good eye contact. Theo was just like me – how could he be Autistic?

As I learned more about neurodivergence, the penny dropped: I had been fed a very narrow view of neurodivergence – autism in particular. I started to uncover answers. But every answer raised more questions and with every question, I felt more and more lost, alone, and confused. The overwhelm was palpable. There was so much information and so much of it was telling me that my child was broken. It was terrifying and heartbreaking and I was so desperate to find someone who understood and could help me make sense of it all.

So, I did what many parents do and I went to people whose job it was to support Neurodivergent kids and their families: education staff, autism experts, and medical professionals. Instead of finding the answers, I was told that the reason my child was so anxious was likely a combination of puberty and flawed parenting. I was told "Yes, he MIGHT be Autistic" but until we had a formal diagnosis (the wait for which was at least two years in our area), I shouldn't "label" him. Rather, the advice was that I needed to show him I wouldn't be manipulated. Make sure he knew who was the boss.

An education professional who I (wrongly) assumed was an "expert" told me that the reason my son didn't want to go to school was that he knew I was "a soft touch". She told me I needed to put my foot down. A CAMHS worker told me that when it came to his anxiety, we needed to teach him to "try harder in the face of adversity". More professionals than I can count told me that Theo needed to "build resilience". I was told that he needed to learn not to interrupt, not to ask so many questions, and not to be so sensitive. I was warned that he was making himself an obvious choice for bullies: Theo needed to try harder to "fit in" and not draw attention to himself.

I was told that my child was broken.

The narrative that accompanied that assertion was that it was almost certainly my fault that my gloriously-Neurodivergent child was struggling.

I now know how ableist, misinformed and harmful that advice was.

This book is the book I needed in those early days – the days when our family was in crisis; when my son's anxiety made him so unwell he couldn't go to school; when I had no idea what sensory needs or emotional regulation or trauma profiles were; when I was blissfully unaware of the damage caused by pervasive stereotypes around neurodivergence; when I was drowning under the weight of well-meaning but incredibly unhelpful advice from professionals who I believed knew what was best for our family; when my only point of reference for autism was Dustin Hoffman's performance in Rain Man. When I had no idea that I too was Autistic!

I hope you find peace and comfort in these pages. I hope you feel seen. Maybe you'll also pick up some tips or gain confidence in your own abilities. Most of all, I hope you'll see in the pages of this book evidence that your child is not broken.

So, come on in. Pull up a chair (or a beanbag . . . or sit on the windowsill . . . or have a bounce on that yoga ball over there . . . or just stand and jiggle about). Hell, take off your bra if you like (assuming you are a bra wearer*)! Take as much or as little of it as feels useful to you.

And please know:

You are welcome here.

You are not alone.

Your child is not broken.

Heidi Mavir
(October 2022)

* Just so you know, I have written this book braless. Yes, as well as being a bit of a potty mouth, I'm also an oversharer.

1

When the Wheels Came
Off in School

Masking, Burnout, and "School Refusal"

Parents of Neurodivergent kids fall into one
of two categories: those for whom a
diagnosis or an identification of need is no
surprise and those of us for whom the
suggestion that our child or young person
might be Neurodivergent hits us like a
speeding night bus, with no headlights on.

I fell into the second category.

Theo loved school. He attended a tiny
village primary. When I say tiny, I mean tiny

– 64 kids in the entire school. He was confident and eager to learn and formed some strong friendships.

When he was nine years old, we moved to a larger city. I knew that the transition would be tricky for Theo: he was going from being a popular kid who knew every other child in a village school, to being the new kid in a massive Primary, with a very different culture. But he settled in well enough and I put any discomfort down to the uncertainty that comes with a house move and change of school.

When Theo progressed to Secondary School, it became clear that even though he had established himself in a friendship group, he still wasn't settled. He told me that school was "too noisy". He told me he felt panicky at break times. He asked for a packed lunch because he didn't like the smells in the canteen. I later discovered that he took to eating his lunch alone in the library and spending most break times hiding out in the toilets, away from the hustle and bustle of a High School with over 2,200 pupils. He told me that the busy corridors made him feel trapped and that he didn't like being jostled up against other students in between lessons. Again, I put it down to him not being used to such a large setting and told myself – and him – he'd get used to it.

Everything came to a head when he started his third year at High School. Halfway through Year 9, his friendship group had an almighty fallout. I still don't know the full details of what happened (let's chalk it down to teenage friendship drama). Regardless of the reason – all of sudden –

Theo's support network disintegrated. The kids he had relied on to find his way to, from, and around school, were gone. It hit him hard. He was devastated at the loss of his friends and, almost overnight, the idea of going to school sent him into a flat spin.

Initially, this presented as a reluctance to get up, then distress at going into the school building on his own (no doubt compounded by the embarrassment of being the only 14-year-old whose mum was walking him to school). Next came tummy aches, headaches, and feeling sick in the mornings. Finally – within a couple of weeks of the friendship fallout – Theo was experiencing full-blown panic attacks. Mornings saw him in floods of tears, clawing at his uniform and begging me not to send him to school. It was horrific.

What followed was my first lesson in how fucked up our school system is. I called the school attendance office:

Attendance Officer (let's call her Karen*): "Hello, Attendance."

Me: "Hi. Yes. I'm just calling to say my son won't be in today."

Karen: "Name?"

Me: "Sorry. What?"

Karen: "Name."

Me: "My name?"

An audible sigh from Karen.

Karen. Slowly, as if speaking to a foreigner. "No. Not your name. Your child's name."

My inner voice: "Of course, not YOUR name, Dingbat!"

Me: with a nervous laugh "Oh. Sorry. Right. Yes. Of course. Theo."

Silence from the other end of the line.

Karen: "Theo . . . ?"

Me: "Yes."

Karen: "And does Theo have a surname?"

Me: "Yes."

My inner voice: "Jesus, Heidi. Why are you like this?"

Karen, with another audible sigh: "And Theo's surname would be . . . ?"

Me: "Shit. Fuck. Sorry."

My inner voice: "I can't believe you just said Fuck."

Me: "It's Bond. Theo Bond."

Karen: "Year Group?"

I was ready for her this time.

Me: "Year 9."

Karen: "And why is he absent?"

Me: "Well . . . he's been having some difficulties. Big fallout with his friends . . . you know how kids are. Anyway . . . I think

14

maybe he's suffering with anxiety or something. He is very upset, you know? Says he doesn't want to come to school."

Karen: "Right. School Refuser?"

Me: "Sorry. What?"

Karen: "He's a school refuser."

Me: "Erm. Is that what it's called? I had no idea that was a thing. Well, he's refusing to come to school so, yes. I suppose so . . ."

My inner voice: "Try to remember to Google 'School Refuser'."

Karen: "Do you have a doctor's note?"

Me: "Erm . . . No. I didn't know I needed one. He's just . . ."

15

Karen: "Without a doctor's note it will be an unauthorised absence."

Me: "Right . . . Sorry. This is all new to me."

Another, much heavier sigh from Karen.

Karen: "You need to bring him in if you don't want an unauthorised absence on his record."

Me: "Sorry. What should I . . ."

Karen: "I'll make a note that you called."

click

* #NotAllKarens — one of my very favourite humans on earth is named Karen. She's sweet and kind and not in any way a knobhead, but I know you know what I mean when I say the woman in the attendance office was a Right Royal Karen and I'm buggered if I remember her actual name, so, Karen, it is.

16

The line disconnected.

And just like that, we clocked up our first "Unauthorised Absence".

The first of many.

* * *

What I didn't know then

1. Masking isn't just a step in painting your skirting boards

Before I knew I had an Autistic child I had only heard the term "masking" once before: the time I ignored my dad's instructions to take time "masking the skirting boards" before painting them. I ended up with gloss paint on my carpets as a result. Once I understood masking, in relation to neurodivergence, it changed my whole way of looking at my and Theo's experiences.

My layman's explanation of Masking:

Neurodivergent people find themselves in a world not built for them. Rather, the world is built to meet the needs of the "majority" neurotypical population. It's thought that around 80% of the world's population is neurotypical (i.e., not Neurodivergent). Places, spaces, and systems have – for the most part – been designed by neurotypical folks for neurotypical folks, often not making allowances for the needs of those of us who are "wired differently". For many Neurodivergent people, the world built for neurotypicals is a challenging place to exist: filled with sensory overwhelm, unintelligible social rules, confusion, and discomfort.

Growing up in a "neuronormative" world, Neurodivergent children are taught from a young age that our way of being is "wrong": "don't rock on that"; "don't fidget"; "don't ask rude questions"; "get down from there"; "stop being silly"; "don't be so sensitive"; "sit still"; "look at me when I'm talking to you." The consequences of us not conforming to neurotypical standards range from being excluded by peers and being "othered" in social situations, to becoming overwhelmed to the point of a meltdown by sensory stimuli and demands on us to do things in a particular way. Many Neurodivergent kids learn early on that not behaving according to neurotypical expectations will result in them getting into trouble and being punished. A natural, unavoidable, and – very often – unconscious consequence of this realisation is that Neurodivergent children "mask" their natural responses, learning to suppress their needs and sensory responses and temper their behaviours. They become experts at "fitting in" as a means of survival.

2. Theo was in Autistic Burnout

It's not uncommon for children and young people who have been identified as Neurodivergent, or who haven't been able to access adequate support, to "hit a wall", after which they are unable to cope in a way they had previously. For many Neurodivergent kids – especially those not formally diagnosed – there can come a point when the wheels come off and their ability to mask in certain environments slips from underneath them.

Sometimes that appears to happen suddenly, as was the case with Theo, who, over six weeks, went from 100% school attendance to not being able to even leave the house. Sometimes those changes in tolerance levels and ability to mask are more gradual – a child or young person might appear to start to find noisy environments too overwhelming. Things that previously didn't seem to bother them become intolerable and distressing over time.

My lovely friend and very clever Neurodivergent Psychotherapist, Kate Jones, explains the impact of Masking like this:

"Masking is known to cause burnout and PTSD in Neurodivergent people and substantially increases the risk of suicide over time. In order to function in a mainstream environment, a child's attempts to mask (to survive) can be traumatic. This contributes to burnout and a decline in self-esteem and mental health."

Regardless of how and when your child hits burnout, the experience is anxiety-inducing and distressing for not only the child or young person, but also for their parents, carers, and other family members.

As I learned about Masking and Autistic Burnout, I came to realise that after our house move, Theo had been under increasing pressure to mask in school. He'd done a great job — we all thought he was "fine in school". He managed to mask his difficulties in school for almost three years. The reality was that he was heading for an almighty crash.

3. "School Refusal" is not uncommon for Neurodivergent kids

I didn't know, back in 2019, that there are thousands of children like Theo, who hit burnout and for whom school becomes an impossible ask. We were told by professionals that our experience was rare. School staff even told me that they didn't know of any other children experiencing similar challenges to Theo. I now know this to be untrue: I have since connected with other parents of children in the same school, who also faced barriers to attendance.

Square Peg – a not-for-profit that works to effect change for children who struggle to attend school – reported that in Autumn Term 2019 (the term when Theo stopped being able to attend school), 921,927 pupils were recorded as "persistently absent" (i.e., more than 10% of sessions missed).

Let that sink in . . . that's almost a million children missing from school!

Now, I know not all of these kids will be Neurodivergent. But recent statistics from the National Pupil Database show that:

> "More than 30% of children who experience school attendance difficulties and become persistently or severely absent have SEND."

Even by conservative estimates, that means that – of the almost one million children and young people who are persistently absent from school – up to (and probably more than) 300,000 of them are kids identified as having Special Educational Needs (SEN).

When I spoke to Ellie Costello from Square Peg, she added:

> "Arguably, this is massively underrepre-
> sented, as any child with emerging needs,

refuted needs, awaiting assessment or who is funnelled down 'behaviour' lens will not be captured in this data."

Even more depressing, post-pandemic stats don't look any better, despite the big push on Attendance following Covid. In the Spring/Autumn term of 2020/21, statistics reported in 'Absence rates by pupil Characteristic', show 42.2% of persistent absentees had a SEN Statement or an EHCP (Education, Health and Care Plan), with a further 16.2% identified as accessing SEN support. Meanwhile, only 7.7% of persistently absent pupils were recorded as not having SEN.

So, kids with additional needs are four times more likely than non-SEN children to experience barriers to attendance.

Theo was NOT a rare case.

Not at all.

The professionals we spoke to almost certainly knew this, especially given the obsession with attendance figures in our school system.

They knew . . . and they didn't tell me.

4. Theo wasn't a "school refuser"

Remember that call with Karen from Attendance, when she told me Theo was a "school refuser"?

Yeah. That's not a thing.

Rather, it's a bullshit piece of parent and child-blaming to draw focus away from the fact a child is struggling and probably has unmet needs. Those of us in the know are pushing back against the term "school refusal", opting instead for "child with barriers to attendance." Why? Because we know that most kids who are healthy and happy and whose needs are being met, LOVE school. Kids who are engaged and who feel safe, skip into school with a thirst for learning adults marvel at.

Theo wasn't a "School Refuser". He told me multiple times that he WANTED to go to school. He would say "I'll try harder" and he DID try. But eventually, it got to the stage when getting into his uniform would see him visibly shaken. Uncontrollable tears would come and he would become so distressed, I genuinely didn't know how to comfort him. Some days I could get him into school. Other days I couldn't even coax him out from under the duvet: he would roll himself into a tiny ball, his face buried into his pile of cuddly toys, apologising in between stifled sobs and repeating over and over "I can't. Mum. I can't."

* * *

Please know

There are thousands of Neurodivergent kids who are struggling either to attend or to just be in school. Your child is not broken. They are trying their best to function in a world not built for them. That's exhausting and a drain on them physically, emotionally, and mentally. It's also a huge strain on you as their primary caregiver.

Once I understood this, I felt empowered to start to push back: when Karen said in our now-daily "chats" that Theo was "refusing" to come to school, I corrected her, saying "he's not refusing, he's too unwell to come to school. Please mark him as ill." When the school SENCO or Principle or Head of Year, used phrases like "he won't come in", "Theo doesn't like coming to school", or "he is refusing to engage" I would remind them that he wasn't being willful or obstructive, but that he was UNABLE to do the things being asked of him. I'd say "it's not won't; it's can't".

Don't get me wrong. This certainly wasn't easy. Some people just didn't want to hear it. When you are an Educational Professional, it is easier to blame a family than consider that your institution might be hurting their children. The shift required to see the truth is just too big a step for lots of people. Despite that, I would encourage you to push back when you know that the words being spoken about your child are not accurate. It's the only way we'll be able to chip away at the narrative that our children are at fault and bring on real change.

Pushing back wasn't an overnight fix but it was the first step toward me learning how to advocate for my child. Knowing that I wasn't making this up and that Theo was not an anomaly, gave me back some power in a situation where I had felt utterly powerless. It was the beginning of a journey of discovery that, ultimately, freed us from the ever-pervasive misunderstanding of neurodivergence that permeates every part of our society.

It was the beginning of me taking back control.

2

Touching the Gate

"Resilience", Behaviour Modification, and Prioritising Your Child's Trust

Worrying about your child messes with your decision-making skills and powers of reasoning. I consider myself a fairly reasonable, intelligent woman. Looking back on some of the things that I was told and the advice I was given in the early days after we realised Theo was probably Autistic, I am astounded by some of the bullshit I swallowed. Astounded, saddened, and ashamed. Hindsight can be a wonderfully painful thing.

One of the words you hear A LOT as a parent of a Neurodivergent child is the word "resilience". The first time this word was used by someone talking about Theo, it came from the mouth of a SENCo after another meeting to discuss Theo's difficulties with attending. A SENCo, or Special Educational Needs Co-Ordinator, is the school teacher responsible for assessing, planning, and monitoring the progress of children with special educational needs and disabilities (SEND). We'll call this one Susi because that was her name.

Susi: "So, the important thing here is to remind Theo that sometimes we have to do things we don't want to do. You know, so that we can help him build resilience."

Me: "Right . . ."

Susi "So, we'll start with you bringing him to school and we'll just ask him to start with touching the gate."

Me: "Touch the gate?"

Susi: "Yes. Let's start with that. That's not too hard."

As I said, I'm not stupid: I do understand the logic behind encouraging him to touch the gate. The theory being that, by breaking down the steps to being back in the school building into smaller, more manageable steps, this "gradual exposure" would help Theo to feel less anxious. Seems fairly reasonable. But – here's the thing – unless this gate had some kind of mystical transformative powers, I knew this wasn't going to work. Because the gate was not the problem. The problem was what was on the other side of the gate. The problem was that Theo was so exhausted from masking that his central nervous system had shut down on him and no amount of gate-touching – regardless of how inviting said gate was – was going to undo that.

I knew that and I think Susi also knew that, but her painted smile and expectant look didn't give me any room to say so.

So, I didn't say "My son is at home unable to leave the house and you want me to manhandle him into the car, drive him to school and perform some kind of fucked up gate-fondling ceremony? For what? So that I can show you – and him – that his feelings aren't important and that he needs to ignore and override his feelings?! So that you can mark him as present on your precious register as attending because he rubbed some railings? You touch the fucking gate, Susi. What a ridiculous idea! We won't be doing that."

I didn't say any of that.

Instead, I said, "Yes, I suppose we could try that."

Susi gave a triumphant nod. For a moment, I wondered if she might be about to give me a reward sticker in recognition of my being so compliant. She trotted off in the direction of the staff room with a cheery wave of her hand and a "See you tomorrow then."

I went home and said to my deeply distressed son "I know this is hard for you

35

but let's just start with touching the gate."

* * *

You may not be surprised to learn that the gate touching was not effective. In fact, it would be fair to say that *Operation Touchgate* was an unmitigated disaster.

We tried it for two weeks. Some days he managed a gate touch, other days, not so much as a railing tickle. He really DID try. We were both committed to the process. Me because I didn't know what else to do and him because he trusted me when I said "All we need to do is touch the gate, then we can go home."

On Day 15, I fucked up.

As we pulled into the car park, I caught sight of him out of the corner of my eye. There he was, my once gloriously-confident boy, crumpled in the seat, his shoulders heaving as he sobbed. I reached out to put my hand on his shoulder for a reassuring rub. He shrugged me off. The sobbing intensified.

"Come on, Mate." I urged, faking confidence "All we need to do is touch the gate. Then we can go home."

He shook his head.

I headed round to his side of the car, opened his door, and took his hand to help him out.

"Come on, Theo. I've got you. You can trust me."

Another shrug. A gentle pull on his arm and he reluctantly climbed out. Once out of the car, his feet were rooted to the spot. I could see that a gate touch wasn't likely today.

"Tell you what," I said, changing tack. "Don't worry about the gate. Let's just walk around the car."

I am not proud of what I did next.

I pressed the button on the key to lock the car.

Theo looked at me. Horror spread across his face. He looked at the locked car. He looked at the gate. He looked back at me. He was shaking by this point, his body gripped by panic.

He swiped his blazer sleeve across his face with a shaky hand.

"Come on, Theo." I repeated "I've got you. You can trust me."

He turned to look me straight in the face "Can I though?" he asked.

A lump rose in my throat.

"Of course," I whispered, not very convincingly.

Then Theo looked me dead in the eye and said "I can't though, can I Mum? I can't trust anyone." Then "What's it going to take for you to listen to me? When will you stop trying to trick me?"

Ouch!

* * *

What I didn't know then

1. "Building Resilience" is professional-speak for "behaviour modification"

When Susi Senco (that's what we're calling her now) first suggested touching the gate, even though it sounded a bit silly to me, I didn't push back. Why? Because a trained education professional, who I had been conditioned to believe was acting in the best interests of my child, suggested it. Talking to other parents since I have come to understand this is a common experience for parents: even when our gut tells us something is off, we don't feel able to say so . . . and we go along with things that – with the benefit of hindsight – we wish we hadn't.

Asking Theo to "just touch the gate" didn't feel like that big a deal. I went along with it because there was logic in the notion of "building resilience". I also went along with it because I was desperately hoping it might help him. I didn't know then that in agreeing to have him touch the gate, I made myself complicit in a programme of Behaviour Modification.

My layman's explanation of Behaviour Modification for Neurodivergent folks:

Based on the idea that Neurodivergent "behaviours" are unwanted and should be prevented, Behaviour Modification works by rewarding wanted, neurotypical behaviour (sitting still, making good eye contact, taking turns, going to school) and punishing or ignoring unwanted, Neurodivergent behaviour (fidgeting, talking too much,

41

displaying distress, not going to school). The hope is that, in time, the subject will stop performing or engaging in unwanted (Neurodivergent) behaviours and instead "choose" wanted (neurotypical) behaviours.

Areas of Behaviour Modification include organised programmes of intervention such as Applied Behavioural Analysis (ABA) and Positive Behaviour Support (PBS), both of which are considered harmful by Neurodivergent-affirming research. Conversion Therapy, Physical Restraint, and Punishment are commonly used as a form of behaviour modification against Neurodivergent children and adults, particularly those housed in institutions. The most extreme is the likes of the Judge Rotenberg Centre in Massachusetts, which uses aversive electric shock devices on Autistic students to discourage unwanted behaviours (yes, really!). Punishment and

Reward programmes can also be seen as Behaviour Modification. "Supernanny", Jo Frost's, The Naughty Step is behaviour modification. More on her later . . .

2. Behaviour Modification encourages Masking

I have no doubt Susi Senco believed she was doing right by Theo with the whole gate-touching business. She maybe even believed that having him touch the gate would, eventually, magically cure him of autism. Honestly, I'm not sure. What I DO know though is that the daily gate encounter's aim was for Theo to expand his window of tolerance to stimulus (in this case, school) so that he could respond to that stimulus in a more "appropriate" way – in this case, by not becoming upset and refusing to go into the school building.

Behaviour Modification seeks to change the person's behaviour, not the environment. The aim of the daily gate fondle was that in time, Theo would learn that school wasn't so bad after all. His behaviour would change and he'd trot back into school ready to continue his education. The gate prodding would present opportunities for him to learn to stop making a fuss, stop being so sensitive, suck it up, and suppress his natural responses to something that was causing him harm. In essence, the gate touching was a lesson in masking.

Building Resilience is never about what is best for the kids we demand it of. Rather, it's about compliance, coercion, and control. It's a means by which we are encouraged to teach our children to mask and it sends them the very clear message again that "fitting in" and not being an inconvenience to other people is more important than their mental or emotional well-being. A phrase I heard that cemented this for me is:

> "No amount of tickling my cheek is going to build sufficient resilience to make me ready to be punched in the face."

The gate touching might have felt like a tap on the cheek but eventually, Theo was going to be expected to take a full punch in the face. And when that face punch came, he was going to be expected to take it on the chin like a man and not make a scene.

3. Relationships trump interventions

The lesson I learned the day Theo questioned whether he could trust me was

painful but necessary. That was the day
that I finally realised that, rather than
letting other people tell me what was best
for Theo, I was going to let him show me.
That was the day we withdrew from
Operation Touchgate. The following
morning, Susi Senco opened an email
from me informing her that we would no
longer be taking part in this particular
intervention, asking that instead, the school
find ways to support Theo that didn't
require me to force him to do something
painful for him and that was damaging to
our relationship. Don't get me wrong, it
didn't go down well. I know for a fact that
I was thought of as one of "those" parents.
Susi Senco and her colleagues believed I
was encouraging Theo's "unwanted
behaviours" with my refusal to buy into
their behaviour modification interventions. I
also know for a fact that my taking a

stand for Theo in this way was a key moment in him knowing that he could indeed trust me. It also saved him from further damage to his mental health that would undoubtedly come with the enforced masking being imposed on him by well-meaning professionals.

* * *

Please know

Just because a person in a position of authority or power suggests an intervention for your child, that doesn't mean you are not allowed to challenge or question them.

Whilst there are some excellent Neurodivergent-affirming professionals, there are also many who believe that neurodivergence is a deficit and a disorder.

Those professionals believe that neurodivergence is a fault and that our Neurodivergent kids are broken. They would much rather we just stopped making a fuss and learned to fit in better. Some of them genuinely believe that our children just need a big dollop of tough love and to be taught that their suffering is less of a priority than — in this case — their school attendance percentages.

That's bullshit.

Your Neurodivergent child doesn't need behaviour modification interventions, designed to "build resilience." There is nobody more resilient than a child who has fought hard to function in a world not built for them. Our kids don't need to be more resilient, any more than they need a punch in the face. Rather, our Neurodivergent children and young people need – and deserve – to be supported by professionals who have an understanding of their differences, compassion for their struggles, and respect for their humanity.

If someone tells you that your Neurodivergent child just needs to "build resilience", tell them to fuck right off.

Prioritising mental health and protecting your relationship with your child is NEVER the wrong decision.

3

Nothing Like Rain Man
The Danger of Stereotypes

Looking back on it – with the knowledge I have now – all the "signs" that Theo was Autistic and ADHD were there. His nursery reports commented on his lack of interest in playing with other children. His singular affection for one, much younger, child was bordering on obsession. He spent hours elbow-deep in lego, building nothing in particular. Theo was also an incessant thumb sucker, he had a preference for sign language over speaking, and was a sensory seeker who was upside down 80% of the time. He NEVER napped during the day.

And yet we missed it.

The reasons we missed it:

1. People have a very narrow and stereo-
   typical view of autism, ADHD, and other
   neurodivergence.
2. Parents aren't open to seeing their children
   as "different", and no one wants to point it
   out.
3. Staff in early years and education settings
   aren't trained in what to look for in identifying neurodivergence.

Before starting on this journey, I had a very
narrow view of neurodivergence. Like many
people, my understanding of autism, in
particular, was largely based on what I'd
seen in the media. In my teens, *Rain Man*
and *What's Eating Gilbert Grape* were huge
Box Office hits. As a result, I thought that

all Autistic people were savants, banged their heads on stuff, and had learning disabilities. Of course, SOME Autistic people do fit those criteria. That's the key though. SOME is not ALL.

Outside of my limited Hollywood-based view of neurodivergence, the only other points of reference I had were from school: a girl in my class called Josephine, who I really liked, and a boy called Graham, who threw chairs. The adults around us described Josephine as "being on the spectrum". She was very quickly moved to a special school. Meanwhile, Graham, who had an ADHD diagnosis, was an absolute fucker. I couldn't stand him.

That was all I had to go on, so I internalised the stereotypes. I developed a view of Neurodivergent people as 'other', 'different', 'weird', and 'abnormal'. Dangerous even.

Is it any wonder that I didn't clock that my child was Neurodivergent? He wasn't like Rain Man or the kid from *Gilbert Grape*; he wasn't like Josephine. He was nothing like Graham. Theo's neurodivergence was hiding in plain sight but my spectacles of misinformed ableist stereotypes wouldn't let me see him.

No one had told me what to look for. Even if they had, I expect I would have dismissed it. After all, Theo was a confident, articulate, chatty toddler. Yes, he struggled with sharing, but then so do lots of little kids. Yes, he preferred the company of adults over other kids his age, but he was living in a single-parent household where most of his interactions were with adults.

Eventually, it was my friend, Char, who helped me to realise that Theo was probably Neurodivergent. Char is a dog person. At the time of writing, Char has 11 dogs of her own and is weaning two litters of puppies. Theo is also a dog person so, when he found out I had a friend with a house full of pooches, he begged me to take him to meet them (the dogs, that is).

It was a warm afternoon in 2019, a couple of weeks into the school summer break, shortly after Theo had started to experience difficulties attending school. We were sitting in Char's garden with a cheeky gin and tonic, watching Theo tumble around the garden in a blur of teenager and fur, living his best life in the company of more dogs than he'd ever been around before.

Char sipped her drink and asked casually "So, how long have you known Theo is Autistic?"

I laughed. I genuinely thought she was joking.

"He's not Autistic," I said, still chuckling.

"Oh . . . OK." was the reply. A beat. Then "Are you sure?"

Over the next couple of hours, I learned more about neurodivergence than I had in the whole of the rest of my life. Char's son, Jack, had been identified as Neurodivergent several years earlier, so she was way ahead of me on her journey. She took the time to help me unpick some of the stereotypes I was harbouring around neurodivergence. Jack wasn't anything like Rain Man either. Rain Man was a fictional character anyway. Jack was also nothing like Josephine or Graham. In fact, Jack was more like Theo than any of the stereotypes I had stored under "A for autism". At first meeting, Jack was a fairly "regular" kid. Jack was also Autistic.

In the weeks that followed, I did what many parents in my position do: I googled the fuck out of anything and everything I could about neurodivergence. My head was spinning, filled with new information about everything from autism to ADHD; Dyslexia to Dyspraxia; Synesthesia to Tourette's Syndrome. Gradually, some of the stereotypes I had been holding onto were chipped away. I started to pick through the truth about neurodivergence. As I did so, it became so bloody obvious. Theo was Neurodivergent!

Once I knew that, the next step was to seek out articles about parenting Neurodivergent kids. I did so in the hope that I would get some more insight into what I was facing. That it might help me make sense of it all. That I might see a way forward for us. I read articles by scholars and researchers who listed all the ways in which Neurodivergent people were "faulty." I read about reduced life expectancy, increased risk of mental health issues, unemployment, and even imprisonment. At one point, I fell into a rabbit hole where people much cleverer than me told me that several high-profile serial killers were probably Autistic. It was pretty grim.

Before long, I found myself neck-deep in content from parents who seemed to be where I was at that moment: full of fear for their children's futures. They spoke of an autism diagnosis being a tragic life sentence. They craved the life enjoyed by "normal" families. They were on a lifelong mission to find therapies, supplements, and interventions to "fix" their broken children.

It was all so utterly depressing. Was this what I was supposed to do now? Spend every waking hour trying to find ways to "fix" Theo?!

* * *

What I didn't know then

1. There is another way

I was fast-approaching total despair when I stumbled upon the writing of Kristy Forbes. Kristy is an Australian-based autism and neurodiversity support specialist. She is parent to four Neurodivergent children. Kristy used vocabulary I hadn't heard before and not just because she was Australian. Kristy talked about *"radical acceptance of neurodivergence"*. Kristy spoke about the damage done to Autistic people's mental health by chasing neuronormative expectations. She wasn't talking about therapies or supplements or interventions: she was talking instead about prioritising relationships with our children and rebelling against the stereotypes being forced on them.

Kristy's words, "radical acceptance", jolted me into the realisation that I needed to give my self-pitying head a good shake.

The penny dropped.

Theo was the same child he had always been. It wasn't Theo who had changed with the realisation that he was Neurodivergent: it was me. I had new information, not a new child. I came to realise that my internalised ableism (which told me there was something "wrong" with neurodivergence) had turned me against my child. My preconceptions, ableism, and fear of disability had set me on a path where I began to see Theo as "other". I looked at him with new eyes, searching for evidence he was broken. I spent hours reading about autism and ADHD and then I made mental tick lists in my head to see just "how Autistic" he was. And in the process, I lost sight of my glorious child.

I realised that I had some choices to make. What kind of parent did I want to be? Did I want to change Theo? Did I want to force him to conform? Did I want to spend the rest of my life in a pit of despair, hoping for a way to "cure" him, pumping him full of overpriced herbal remedies from the internet? Or did I want to find a way to support him, celebrate him, and love him for all that he was?

I opted for the latter.

2. My son wasn't a stereotype any more than your child is

The biggest step towards becoming the parent I wanted to be was facing and challenging my ignorance.

When we are faced with the realisation that our children are of a minority neurotype, and we are trying to make sense of it, it's natural to look to other families for similarities with our own. The danger is that we are then sucked into a rabbit hole of stereotypes, which dehumanise our children and throw a veil over our ability to see them as individuals. Staying connected to your child and reminding yourself that they haven't changed will serve you well.

I know now that no two Neurodivergent people are the same because no two humans are the same. Being around other parents showed me what I now know to be true:

> "When you've met one Neurodivergent person, you've met ONE Neurodivergent person."

3. Unpicking ableism can be a tricky process

When I first read the word "ableism", I had an immediate defensive response. I considered myself a tolerant, loving human being and was offended at the idea that I might be carrying some ableist views, opinions, and stereotypes. I thought that ableism meant going out of your way to discriminate against disabled people. I had never done that. Turns out I had a pretty narrow view of what disability is and hadn't really understood what ableism was either.

The Equality Act defines Disability as;

> "a physical or mental impairment that has
> a 'substantial' and 'long-term' negative
> effect on your ability to carry out normal
> day-to-day activities."

(Equality Act 2010)

Long-term, in terms of the Equality Act, means more than 6 months. Day-to-day activities include things like going to school, travelling, and self-care tasks.

Medical News says Ableism;

> "hinges on the idea that people with
> disabilities are less valuable than non-
> disabled people."

"All good," says me. "Disability doesn't just mean wheelchair users and ableism doesn't just mean being a dick to wheelchair users. Got it. I still don't think I'm ableist."

But there's more.

In 2007, a US study of 2.5 million respondents found that 76 per cent of respondents (including disabled respondents) showed an unconscious bias for people without disabilities. The writers of the study go on to state that while;

> "nearly all of us have implicit biases, we can take steps to minimize how often they are activated and how much they affect our perceptions, decisions, and actions. The first step is to acknowledge that all of us have implicit biases despite our egalitarian intentions and learn about

the . . . influence of implicit biases on our
judgment, decisions, and actions."

Our world is built for the majority, and the
majority are not disabled. We are conditioned
to favour the majority and to try to
conform to majority standards. As a result,
the tendency is for society as a whole to
lean toward the medical model of disability.
The medical model of disability says people
are disabled by their impairments or
differences. Under the medical model,
impairments or differences should be "fixed"
by medical and other interventions. The
alternative is the social model of disability.
The social model of disability says that
disability is caused by the way society is
organised and that disabled people are best
supported when efforts are made to support
and accommodate them, rather than "fix"
them.

"Ah!" Says me. Cue the sound of another penny dropping.

I have come to realise it's important to acknowledge that we are all operating under majority rule: of our laws, our systems, and our institutions. Acknowledging and understanding that is the first step towards freeing ourselves from the unconscious bias and ableist beliefs that turn us against our own children. Of course, not ALL impacts of a person's disability are down simply to the world around them. Not for a second am I denying that life for disabled people can be incredibly difficult but once I was able to grasp the fact that unconscious bias was at play inside my head, it freed me from imposing all those stereotypes on my child.

* * *

Please know

Deciding to push back against stereotypes and challenge your own unconscious bias is an act of courage. Adopting the social model of disability will serve you and your child better than clinging to the medical model.

Your child is still (and always will be) the glorious human they have always been. You are allowed to cut yourself some slack when realising you've been carrying around the burden of ableist nonsense. Doing so will free you from neuronormative expectations of what you "should" be doing, and enable you to move forward and be intentional about the kind of parent you want to be.

Becoming a "rebel parent" by deciding to be radically accepting of your child's neurodivergence will go some way to protecting your child from unnecessary harm. Loving them fiercely, whilst strengthening your understanding of their particular needs will also model to your child – and the people around them – the importance of them being seen as an individual. You are allowed to decide to swim against the tide. In doing so, you will free yourself and your child from the weight of ableist expectations and stereotypes. Your child deserves that.

4

"Why Would You Want to Label Your Child?"

The Diagnosis Dilemma

Despite describing my child's difficulties to education and health professionals, despite asking for support, despite telling people that Theo was Autistic, I was met time and time again with "he doesn't have a formal diagnosis though, does he?" Repeatedly, the lack of formal diagnosis was used as an excuse to not provide support. It was also used to gaslight me and to call into question my parenting and his mental well-being. In one meeting a professional suggested that I was "encouraging Autistic behaviours" by telling Theo I believed he was Neurodivergent. I was told, "If you believe he's Autistic it will become a self-fulfilling prophecy". As if being Autistic was a) performative and b) THE worst thing in the world.

After waiting almost a year for an assessment, we were finally seen by our local Diagnostic service. Turns out, Theo didn't do a convincing job of being "Autistic enough" in the assessments (hello, masking!) and it was decided that he did not meet the criteria for a diagnosis. The assessing professional appeared disappointed at Theo's response when she told him.

"If I'm not Autistic, what is it then?" he asked. His frustration was clear.

Her answer was "autism is a disability."

"Yeah. I know," said Theo.

"You don't want to be disabled, do you?" she asked.

Oh, hello there, ableism!

It would take another three years and a private assessment for us to FINALLY get a formal autism diagnosis.

Theo cried all the way home.

* * *

On 12 October 2022, TV's SuperNanny, Jo Frost (yes, she of behaviour modification Naughty Step fame) posted an image on social media. The text overlaid read:

"*Today in the 21st Century people want to banish the word "NAUGHTY". They say it is a negative word to describe a child's behaviour. Yet we want to desperately LABEL our children ADD, ADHD, ODD, and every other ABCD.*"

There was a significant backlash from the SEND Community with parents reminding Jo that stating that parents of Neurodivergent children are "desperate to label" and that behaviours in Neurodivergent kids are a "choice" is deeply offensive. The fact a "parenting expert" felt confident enough in her view to choose the phrase "and every other ABCD" is telling. Even more telling though is the support she received from people on social media agreeing with her position. It was a clear illustration of wider society's misunderstanding, ableist judgments and assumptions about our children.

For me, being able to finally claim the "labels" of Autisic and ADHD in my 40s, was a game changer. The day I got my formal diagnosis (aged 47) I sobbed with relief – FINALLY a "label" that fit. The relief was because until I knew that I was Autistic and ADHD, I carried the burden of inaccurate labels, pinned on me by other people: I was labelled "lazy", "scatty", "disorganised", "oversensitive", "unreliable", "fidgety", "a daydreamer", "manic", "over the top", "a rottweiler", "scary", "rude", "blunt", "inconsiderate", "unfriendly", "crazy", "messy", "weird".

All the while I didn't know that I was Neurodivergent, those labels carried such stigma and shame for me: they told me that there was something "wrong" with me. That I needed to "fix" myself. That I was broken. And when some of the same words were used to describe my child, they told me the same things about him.

* * *

What I didn't know then

1. Diagnosis is a privilege

On average, it takes three and a half years to secure an autism diagnosis in the UK. It's two years for an ADHD diagnosis.

Many people, even if they can pursue a diagnosis, may be hindered by preconceptions and bias from referrers and assessing professionals, which are further barriers to formal diagnosis. It is well documented that children from marginalised racial groups are identified later than their white peers, if they are ever identified at all. Research by AMJ Public Health from 2009 found that;

74

"among children meeting the case definition of ASD . . . children who were Black, Hispanic, or of other, non-White ethnicities were less likely than were White children to have documentation of an ASD in their records. For Black children, this disparity persisted regardless of their known IQ; for Hispanic and Asian children, the disparity was concentrated among those with intellectual disability. These findings are in line with previous research showing that Black children with ASD are diagnosed at older ages than are White children and that Hispanic children are less likely than are White children to be diagnosed with ASD at all."

Racial/Ethnic Disparities in the Identification of Children With Autism Spectrum Disorders.

We also know that children and young people who are identified, or socialised as, males are three times more likely to be diagnosed as Autistic than those identified, or socialised as, females. A 2017 analysis of multiple data sources by Rachel Loomes, Laura Hull and William Polmear Locke Mandy found;

> *"There appears to be a diagnostic gender bias, meaning that girls who meet criteria for ASD are at disproportionate risk of not receiving a clinical diagnosis."*
>
> What Is the Male-to-Female Ratio in Autism Spectrum Disorder? A Systematic Review and Meta-Analysis 2017.

Cambridge University Research has found that Trans, Non-binary and gender non-conforming children and young people, are statistically more likely to be Autistic. Trans and Non-binary Autistics also have significant barriers to accessing healthcare, due to institutionalised transphobia and a lack of understanding of gender issues in the wider clinical community.

Diagnosis is a privilege not afforded or accessible to all.

2. Labels are Care Instructions

Labels are not a bad thing when they serve a purpose. If you think about clothing, for example, a label on a garment is a care instruction. So long as someone knows how to read a label and knows what the different icons on a laundry label mean, they can make sure that they don't ruin clothes by putting them in a washer on the wrong cycle.

Knowing that a child is a handwash only, don't tumble dry, delicate mohair jumper, who you will destroy if you throw them in the washer with your bed sheets on a hot wash, is useful information.

People have labelled my child all his life. I would far rather have a label that is accurate and that "batches" him with other incredibly Neurodivergent people who are like him: who he can feel a kinship with. I am hopeful that when he tells people that he is Autistic, that might also be an opportunity for education. People might stop and think "I need to know a bit more about that" and that might help us start to dismantle some of the dangerous, ableist stereotypes we have about neurodivergence.

3. Disability is not a dirty word

In 2017, a new strategy to empower disabled people was rolled out in the UAE.

Part of that was a proposed "rebranding" of disabled people and guidance to use the term "People of Determination" rather than "Disabled People". I have questions: Are we only valuable as humans if we are also "determined"? How determined do we need to be in order to be considered important? How do you judge "determination?" What happens if we're just tired or too unwell to demonstrate our determination to overcome our challenges?! People of Determination? How flipping patronising!

Some people don't think we should use the term "disabled" to identify ourselves or our children. It's a label they don't feel comfortable with. Because, for them, nothing would be worse than being or becoming disabled. Literally the definition of ableism.

I want to encourage you to not be frightened of the word disabled. Once you embrace the social model of disability over the medical model and acknowledge that we are disabled primarily by society's preconceptions of us, the word "disabled" is no longer a value judgment on us as individuals. Disabled doesn't mean broken. It doesn't mean faulty. It isn't an invitation to use our determination to make "inspirational videos" on social media.

Disability means – quite simply – "this person may need accommodations." Disabled is a descriptive term that highlights the challenges we face in a world not built for us. Rather than changing the word, I want to challenge people to change the way they view disability. I use the word to describe myself and my child and I don't shy away from it.

* * *

Please know

There can be power in pointing out to people that your Neurodivergent child is disabled. As a disabled person, your child is protected from discrimination by laws (both in the UK and in the US). Reclaiming the word and the "labels" that others are so frightened by is a really powerful way to cut through the cloud of ableist prejudgements some folks have about neurodivergence.

5

Discomfort is the Price of Admission to a Meaningful Life

Now That's What I Call Ableist Gaslighting Volume 5

Trigger warning for this chapter – mention of childhood sexual abuse.

I recently supported the family of a 7-year-old Autistic child in their fight for support. We'll call her Poppy. Poppy's long list of diagnoses included (but was not limited to) visual impairment, autism with a Pathological Demand Avoidance (PDA) Profile, and ADHD. She was also being treated for an eating disorder. Poppy had been deeply traumatised by attempts to integrate her into an educational environment and had been out of school for almost three years. An Educational Psychologist (EP) was brought in to assess Poppy and make recommendations for her education.

Now, I've seen a lot of reports, both from education and health professionals and I will admit that I usually have to take deep breaths when reading them. It can be difficult to read reports written by professionals whose practice is rooted in neuronormativity. Often the wording in these reports pathologises and dehumanises the children and young people they speak about. Reports are packed full of ableism, parent blaming, and dismissal of Neurodivergent experiences. I've learned to breathe through it, but even I was given reason to pause when I read one particular sentence in this report. The phrase was:

"*Discomfort is the price of admission to a meaningful life.*"

The quote is taken from a TedTalk by Dr. Susan David, in which she explains the importance of not suppressing our feelings. The TedTalk is pretty good – do go look it up. However, this EP used this quote, out of context, to justify several behaviour modification goals for this <u>7-YEAR-OLD</u> Neurodivergent child, including:

"*Needs to learn to engage with activities that are not of her choosing*

Needs to be able to tolerate not knowing and learning about things that she finds uninteresting

*Needs to be able to cope when things do
not turn out as she hoped*

Needs to be able to play imaginatively

*Would benefit from learning about
conversation being two-way and being
able to hear someone else's story"*

And – finally – this corker:

"Needs to learn to be flexible in thought"

I mean . . . she could have saved her word
count and gone for a simple:

"Poppy needs to stop being so Autistic."

Just in case there was any doubt as to this
professional's opinion that it is the child
who should change, not the environment,
she rounded off with;

> "The temptation will be to remove the
> stimulus causing the difficulty however
> this will be detrimental to Poppy's
> learning and ability to cope with the world
> as it is."

Fucking yikes!

Unfortunately, this isn't a one-off. I recently asked members of my Facebook community to share with me things that had been said to them about their Neurodivergent children. Over 100 comments later and I was inspired to compile a list of some of the ignorant, ableist bullshit said to parents of Neurodivergent kids by adults who seem to believe disabled children just need to try harder. These are all direct quotes from professionals.

Radio jingle plays

"Welcome, Pop Pickers! Here, for your delectation and delight is this week's Top Ten of Fuckery Parents Have Endured . . .

In at Number Ten, a new entry from Swedish mega-group, ABA, it's the timeless classic, "Don't Let Him Control You."

At Number Nine the newest release from Justin Comprehensible "How About We Leave the Autism at the Door?"

Holding their position at Number Eight is thrash mental megastars, Resilience, with "They Won't be Able to Use Ear Defenders in The Workplace."

At Number Seven, it's the ever-popular floor filler "If He Could Just Take Turns" by Cher.

Number Six is the power ballad that's been climbing up the charts for weeks "You need to Reward Positive Communication" from Bea Quiet and The Sensory Seekers.

Sliding in at Number Five, "Wrapping Her Up In Cotton Wool Won't Do Her Any Favours" by AdamAnt, showing us all that the old ones are indeed the best.

"He's Doing That On Purpose" by The Professionals is Number Four this week.

Climbing this week from twelve, into Number Three, it's "Could You Make Life At Home Less Comfortable?" by Go Outside.

Straight in at Number Two "The World Won't Change for Them" by Boy Band The Fit Ins, taken from their Platinum selling Album, "Time for a Parenting Course".

And topping the Charts at Number One, for the 67th Week, beating the record previously held by Susi Senco, is "Set Some Boundaries" by Rod Foryourownback.

Join us next week for another weekly countdown of the charts, brought to you in association with Absolute Cobblers – Footwear for All Occasions."

* * *

What I Know Now

1. **When it comes to providing support for Neurodivergent families, there is an embedded culture of ableism, parent blame, and professional gaslighting.**

Institutionalised parent blame in the UK was considered such a significant problem by leading charity Cerebra, they commissioned a large piece of research in 2021. The research looked into families' experiences of dealing with Local Authority Children's Services. The research found that;

> "most English Children's Services Authorities operate a 'one-size-fits-all' approach to families – regardless of whether it is a parent carer seeking support for a disabled child or a family where the evidence suggests there to be neglect or abuse. The effect of this approach is to create an institutional culture of 'parent blame'."
>
> Institutionalising Parent-carer Blame, Cerebra 2021.

Cerebra says that parents find the process of dealing with local authorities "humiliating, intimidating and bullying".

Parents are often gaslit during our interactions with professionals and support services. When this happens the professional in question manipulates (gaslights) you to the point that you question your own sanity, memory, or perceptions. Typical gaslighting techniques include denying or questioning your child's neurodivergence, downplaying the impact of their challenges, or even retelling events so that you take the blame. Gaslighting can look like being told that you are mollycoddling your child or being told that they are "fine" when you aren't there. It's implied (or even explicitly stated) that the only people letting our children down is us, their parents.

When I experienced outright ableism and professional gaslighting for the first time, I was taken aback. It really knocked my confidence to have a professional tell me that Theo needed to "try harder to cope in the real world" and to be told, "he will be picking up on your anxiety." It made me question myself. Was I being oversensitive? Was I a pushover? Maybe I wasn't helping him and did just need to suck it up and apply some tough love? All these people, who had way more experience than I did, couldn't all be wrong, could they? Before I knew it, I was nodding and agreeing. They were right. I was a shit parent. I was the problem and I was making things worse for my child.

But then I came to realise that – like hundreds (probably thousands) of parents like me – I was falling foul of a system that subscribes to stereotypes and the medical model of disability. What's more, the ableism around neurodivergence means there is an extra level of bullshittery whereby the approach taken to supporting our children often rides on what's convenient for the majority, not about what's in the best interest of the minority.

Perhaps the hardest part of professional gaslighting for me was realising that it was so much a part of the "system", that professionals themselves didn't even realise they were doing it. Unintentional gaslighting happens when the offender does not know that they are gaslighting a person. When challenged, they are being honest when they say they haven't done it, because they don't see it in their actions. Although the unintentional gaslighter has no intent to harm, their statements do end up harming their victim. When it comes to gaslighting, intention does not reduce impact.

2. Ableism against Neurodivergent people is next-level bullshit

There's an added level of complexity that comes with ableism around neurodivergence. Not to play down the impact of ableism on other disabled folks in the least – ableism is crappy for anyone. However, this idea that we have to "push past" our disability seems to be levelled at Neurodivergent people more than those with other disabilities. Most folks can see that it wouldn't be appropriate to suggest to a wheelchair user at the bottom of a set of stairs that they "just get up and give it a go" or tell a Deaf person to "try listening harder". By the same token, most of us are not ignorant enough to tell parents of a child with physical impairments that they will need to overcome their disability to have a meaningful life. Yet, every day, professionals do just this.

They expect – or even demand – that Neurodivergent children do the impossible: be neurotypical. What's more, these same professionals believe that it's acceptable that our kids endure significant pain, discomfort, and distress in order to do so.

Author Alexander Den Heijer put it beautifully when he said;

"When a flower doesn't bloom, you fix the environment in which it grows, not the flower."

We must be able to remind ourselves of this because the alternative is that we then gaslight ourselves into ignoring the very real needs of our children and, as a result, professionals dictate harmful approaches which encourage masking and damage our children.

3. Consent matters

In the UK, Control and Coercive behaviour against a person over 16 is a crime. Controlling behaviour is defined by the Crime Prosecution Service as;

> "a range of acts designed to make a person subordinate and/or dependent by isolating them from sources of support, exploiting their resources and capacities for personal gain, depriving them of the means needed for independence, resistance and escape and regulating their everyday behaviour."

Unfortunately, our children are not protected by this law. As minors, they have very few rights. Our children are subjected to "interventions" and approaches suggested by professionals that, in another context, would be considered controlling and coercive practices. This matters particularly for Neurodivergent children and young people and not JUST because we know that masking is harmful. For me, there's a bigger issue here – and that's the issue of consent.

Let's go back to the original statement from that delightfully gaslighting Educational Psychologist who stated that *"Discomfort is the price of admission to a meaningful life"*. What message are we sending to our Neurodivergent children and young people if we take this approach? We are teaching them that they must do what they are told and comply with adult instructions and expectations, regardless of how painful they find it. We are telling them that their discomfort comes second to the wants and needs of other people. We are teaching them to put up and shut up. Most worrying of all, we are showing them that even if they find something painful, they must submit to adults.

We are teaching our children that their consent doesn't matter and – in doing so – we are making them incredibly vulnerable. As an undiagnosed Autistic child, I didn't know that I was allowed to say No. I was never given the opportunity to know that I could grant or withdraw consent. For me personally, that was disastrous. I was sexually assaulted at eight years old by a friend's older brother and again at 15 by a much older man at a family wedding. I had been taught not to question adults. Not to be rude. I was raised to not make a fuss. I didn't know that I could say no. I didn't tell anyone about the abuse until I was in my 30s.

* * *

Please know

If you are feeling that you are being blamed and gaslighted, you're unlikely to be imagining it. Professional parent blaming is incredibly common. You are allowed to question and challenge professionals, regardless of how sure they seem that their opinion is right. Experts should "be on tap, but not on top."

It's especially difficult to read these documents when they are about your own child.

The wheelchair-user analogy can be helpful when challenging ableism against Neurodivergent people.

We must model consent to our Neurodivergent children. They – and you –

are allowed to say No. You are also allowed to say "I don't know", "I'm not sure", "Not right now" or nothing at all. None of those phrases should be read as consent.

A "Yes" secured with coercion, control, gaslighting and the need to mask, is NOT consent. You and your child deserve to know that our brains, bodies, and lives are our own. Consent should never be assumed.

Dr. Susan David (who delivered the TedTalk that Poppy's EP lifted and twisted the quote from to fit their own agenda) says this:

"When emotions are pushed aside or ignored, they get stronger". She adds *"Diversity isn't just people, it's also what's inside people. Including diversity of emotion."*

Your Neurodivergent child might have "big" feelings. Bigger than other children their age even. They are not broken and they definitely don't need to have those big feelings trained out of them.

6

The Apple Doesn't Fall Far From the Tree

The Domino Effect of Discovering My Child's Neurodivergence

One of the things that Theo asks me a lot is "how did you not realise I was Autistic?" We'll be chatting and I'll say something like "When you were a baby you HAD to be rocked to sleep" or "you used to empty the penny jar and line up a snake of coins on the rug." And he'll look at me and say "Bloody hell, mother! How did you not know?"

For a long while, I had no answer for him.

Until – during a phone call with Kristy Forbes – I had another penny-drop moment. The following is the retelling of that conversation as my brain remembers it, complete with hilarious references to Kristy being Australian.

Kristy: "G'Day Mate" (She's Australian. Did I mention that?) "How's it going?"

Me: "I've been better. I am feeling so guilty. Theo keeps asking me why it took so long for me to realise he was Autistic and I feel like I don't have a satisfactory answer for him."

Kristy: "Yeah. That can be rough."

Me: "Like, I know it's down to stereotypes and lack of training for professionals being a barrier to identification but . . ."

Kristy: "Yeah?"

Me: "All the way through this process, I have had this awful guilt because I didn't see Theo's neurodivergence. That somehow I refused to admit that he might be 'different'."

Kristy: "Is he 'different'?"

Me: "Well, not really. Not to me."

Kristy: "He's not different to you?"

Me: "No."

Kristy: "He's a lot like you?"

Me: "Yeah. He's very like me."

Kristy: "Isn't that interesting?"

Me: "Yeah."

Kristy: "He's Autistic and he's very like you . . ."

Me: "Yeah."

Kristy: "Yeah . . ."

Me: "Shit. I'm Autistic."

Kristy, laughing: "Ya think?"

Long silence while Kristy waits for me to process this mind-blowing revelation.

Me: "Shit. Wow. Is that why every time I read something about neurodivergence, I'm like . . . God, that sounds a lot like me."

Kristy: "Fun fact. Very few neurotypical people spend any time wondering if they might be Neurodivergent."

Another, slightly shorter, silence for more processing.

Me: "Right. Well, thanks for not telling me I'm probably making it up."

Kristy: "You are very welcome."

Me: "Shit. Wow!"

Kristy: "Don't worry. We've got you. Ya great galah." (Uber Australian, you see)

* * *

There was nothing notable to me about the way Theo "presented" as a child because I "presented" very similarly. For me, there was nothing noteworthy about a child who was very anxious in social situations and found friendships difficult, because that was my experience too. It was nothing out of the ordinary for me to have a child who puts their hands over their ears when hand dryers go off, or a plane goes overhead. I did the same (as did my younger brother). It made total sense to me that Theo liked to be upside down because I love being upside down too. Like him, I slept under three duvets; I HATED having my hair washed and would scream my way through bath times; I was obsessed with my toy kaleidoscope and spent many an hour elbow-deep in lego. It made sense to me – and I didn't think it was anything other than completely regular that Theo sang himself to sleep because I did that for years too.

Turns out my apple didn't fall far from my tree at all.

* * *

What I didn't know then

1. **If a child is Neurodivergent, there is a good chance, one or other of their biological parents is too**

Since the 70s, scientists have carried out studies to establish the heritability of autism and other neurodivergence. The general consensus of the studies undertaken is that if you have a sibling or child with an autism diagnosis, you are statistically significantly more likely to also meet the criteria for a diagnosis. We now understand that neurodivergence is an inheritable difference in brain function and structure and nervous system function and structure.

We also know from research that neurodivergence is not something that you "catch" – it is a neurological difference, not an infectious disease. You definitely don't get it from the MMR vaccine. In 1988 Andrew Wakefield claimed that the MMR caused autism. This was proved to be untrue. What's more, it was later proved to be a fraudulent claim, made by Wakefield and his team for personal financial gain. Andrew Wakefield was consequently struck off by the British Medical Council.

Once more for the folks at the back: <u>THE MMR VACCINE DOES NOT CAUSE AUTISM.</u>

A large number of the parents of Neurodivergent children who I have supported have come to question whether they too might also be Neurodivergent. They have their own "apple doesn't fall far from the tree" lightbulb moments as they learn more about neurodivergence. Some folks might argue that that's because parents of Neurodivergent kids are "looking for it". That it's confirmation bias. That doesn't ring true to me. To me, it makes absolute sense that my child would have a similar neurotype, nervous system, and way of showing up in the world to me. It would be weirder if they didn't. Even if confirmation bias was at play, that doesn't explain the number of adults who go on to be diagnosed as Neurodivergent after their children have been identified.

Most of the information out in the public domain about autism is focused on childhood presentation. If you are looking at your Neurodivergent child and thinking "I can't see the similarities with me", this is your gentle reminder that Autistic kids grow up

to be Autistic adults, just as allistic
(non-Autistic) kids grow up to be allistic
adults. Expecting your adult experiences
and presentation to be similar to your
child's, is like expecting a neurotypical
grown-up to behave like a four-year-old.
Many late-identified Neurodivergent folks
have found coping strategies and have
been masking for years. That, combined
with the fact we are no longer children,
means that we don't "fit" the infantilised
picture many of us have of neurodivergence.
When, as an adult, we are faced with the
notion that we might be Autistic, we often
talk ourselves out of it because we are
measuring ourselves against what autism in
children looks like, not what autism in
adulthood looks like.

If you're reading this and thinking "Oooh.
Interesting. My kid is Neurodivergent and

I think my partner is too." I have a little extra cat to throw amongst the pigeons. In the same way, as Neurodivergent parents have Neurodivergent kids, Neurodivergent folks often couple with other Neurodivergent folks. So yes, there is a good chance that the other parent of your Neurodivergent child is Neurodivergent. There's also a pretty good chance that you are too! I'm not here to amateur diagnose you. I just want to share that – sometimes – in the domino effect of realisations about neurodivergence, ours is the last domino in the line. I identified a shedload of Autistic people around me (including the father of my child, my parents, my cousins, aunts, uncles, grandparents, and nephews) before the penny dropped that I was Neurodivergent too.

2. Realising that you might be Neurodivergent can take a bit of processing

After recovering from the initial shock of my penny drop moment, what followed swiftly after was a whole lot of big feelings.

I experienced a cascade of feelings that swung from confusion to anger to grief. Understanding my neurodivergence gave me a new lens through which to see my personal history. I felt like I was going back over the events of my life and re-filing them. I was 45 when I realised I was Autistic. My ADHD diagnosis came when I was 47 years. Over 40 years of not understanding myself. 40 years of thinking that other people thought I was weird and not knowing why. Countless therapy sessions, CBT, and self-help books, all in a bid to understand what was "wrong" with me. The cost to my mental health was significant.

For me, there was a freedom that came with realising I was Neurodivergent. Finally, a "label" that made sense. There was also sadness. I mourned all the missed opportunities. I felt sorrow when thinking about how different my life could have been. I grieved the years I had spent believing that I was broken.

3. Self-Identification is valid

Making the connection and realising that I was also Neurodivergent put me in a rather strange position. I spent a lot of time wondering if maybe I was just telling myself that to let myself off the hook. After all, when I previously asked my doctor for a referral to the services responsible for adult diagnosis in my area, they discharged me, stating that I "Was well presented and articulate. Made good eye contact. Has a successful career and is functioning well." Turns out that after 45 years, I was really good at masking, despite trying REALLY hard not to mask in the assessment. They also added "Presents as having a Personality Disorder. May benefit from anti-anxiety medication." No shit, Sherlock!

It made me question myself. If I wasn't neurotypical enough to manage in a neurotypical world, but I also wasn't Autistic enough to get referred for an assessment, where did that leave me? I was stranded in a weird no man's land where, everywhere I looked, I still felt like an outsider. It was Kristy Forbes who assured me that self-identification is valid within the Neurodivergent community.

Whilst professionals seem to be mildly to severely obsessed with "formal diagnosis", people who have experienced the nightmare that is trying to secure an assessment know that diagnosis is a privilege. As such, it is widely accepted within the Autistic and Neurodivergent Communities that self-ID is valid. We tend to use the words "identified as Autistic" or "recognised as ADHD" rather than "diagnosed with ASD". I did go on to decide to pursue a private diagnosis. I know that I am fortunate to have been able to do so. I also know, in terms of being accepted and acknowledged within the Neurodivergent community, that was not necessary. I have never been asked by someone within the Autistic Community if I am "officially diagnosed." That was such a relief and a comfort to me and I hope it will be to you too.

* * *

Please know

It's ok to not be ready to consider that you might be Neurodivergent. It's also ok to allow yourself time to consider that you may be. Regardless of which route you pursue – and when – it will take some processing. Take as much time as you need. You deserve to have people around you who will support you whilst you work through the questions you have about your own neurotype. You don't owe anyone an explanation or a piece of paper that shows you have been able to convince a diagnostician that you meet the very limited criteria laid out for a formal diagnosis in the DSM V (the "handbook" for diagnosing autism and other conditions).

Feeling an affiliation with other Autistic folks – and recognising Autistic traits in yourself – is enough for you to be accepted by the Neurodivergent community. Most of us understand that diagnosis is a privilege not accessible or necessary for everyone. If you tell one of us that you or your child are Neurodivergent, you won't need to disclose if you have a formal diagnosis. As far as most of us in the Neurodivergent Community are concerned, when you tell one of us that you think you are one of us, then you are one of us.

7

I Might Kill Myself

The Personal Cost of Keeping It All Together

Trigger warning for this chapter – discussion of mental health, depression, suicidal ideation and alcohol misuse.

It's the day before Christmas Eve 2019. I am in my GP's office. I am out of bed for the first day in almost three weeks. I am in my pyjamas with a big coat thrown over the top. I have boots on my feet, without socks. My hair is unbrushed. I am sure I smell awful. I know that I look like shit. I am sobbing uncontrollably.

I have just told Dr. Bolder that I am here because I am frightened that I might be about to hurt myself and my son. I can't think clearly. I struggle to string the words together. I don't tell her that yesterday I drove on the motorway at ninety miles an hour without a seatbelt on, unable to see properly because the tears wouldn't stop. I don't tell her that I contemplated smashing into the lorry beside me. I don't tell her that the only thing that stopped me was the realisation that I couldn't leave my son with no one to care for him. I can't bring myself to tell her that my new plan was to work out how to kill myself and take him with me.

The doctor is amazing. In between my sobs, I hear her in a soft, gentle tone say "It's ok. I'm going to help you."

* * *

What I didn't know then

1. Poor mental health and mental health diagnoses often co-occur with Neurodivergence

To say that poor mental health has been something I have always struggled with feels like the understatement of the century. I am what can be described as a person with "all the feelings all the time." I was a highly sensitive and extremely anxious child. I was an incredibly hormonal and lonely teenager. My Mum died when I was nineteen. My twenties are a blur of grief and depression. I sobbed and drank my way through my 30s.

I've had a variety of diagnoses, from your common or garden Generalised Anxiety and Persistent Depressive Disorder, to the delightfully titled Borderline Personality Disorder. Most recent was the suggestion that I would probably meet the criteria for a complex PTSD diagnosis. I have been on and off medication for my mental health since my late teens. Before this, I had had two other times in my life when I have been suicidal. It's been quite a ride.

Alongside medication, I've had a LOT of therapy, with mixed success. I've had talking therapy hypnotherapy, CBT, and variations thereof. I even trained in CBT and qualified as a Mental Health First Aider in a bid to better understand what might be going on inside my head.

Whilst it made sense to me when professionals explained that I was suffering from poor mental health, it always felt like there was something amiss in my diagnoses. Yes, I was anxious. Yes, I was depressed. Yes, the fear of being alone was all-consuming on occasion. Yes, I experienced flashbacks to childhood trauma . . . but I had a sense that there was something else.

Now, I'm not saying that I didn't have mental health challenges. I am not ashamed of my diagnoses and, for the most part, they do make sense, I just always had a feeling that there was something else going on. Therapy was helpful on occasion but it felt like it missed the mark a lot of the time. The experiences I had in therapy whilst trying to unpack and unpick my mental health left me feeling more confused, ashamed, frightened, and frigging exhausted. Something didn't add up. I would sit in appointments, going through the motions, with a little voice inside my head saying "If only they knew how broken you really are." Sometimes a therapist would explain something to me and I would nod along, even though what they had explained just didn't feel true for me. I was too scared to tell anyone how I was feeling. I didn't want to upset anyone by telling them that every session I had just confirmed what I already believed – that my brain wasn't like everyone else's.

I concluded that there must be something desperately wrong with me. I was definitely broken.

That day in the doctor's office was a turning point. At this point, I was still pootling around with the idea that I might be Autistic but I was pushing it to one side to allow me the brain space I needed to deal with other things. It had been three months since we had FINALLY got some education provision in place for Theo and in the weeks since, I had slipped into an exhausted depression that refused to lift.

Dr. Bolder asked me some pretty direct questions about my suicidal thoughts. Did I have specific plans for ending my life? Who had I shared this with? What did we need to do to keep me safe whilst I was experiencing these thoughts and feelings? And – finally – what did I know about Burnout? And there it was. That all-important connecting word. She didn't mention autism or neurodivergence. She didn't need to. I knew what Burnout was. And at that moment I knew that's where I was.

I realised later that the reason I had felt so "out-of-touch" with so much of the therapy I had had, was because, throughout the process, I had thought I was neurotypical.

For the most part, my therapists had too. Everything was delivered through a neurotypical lens, which was why I felt so disconnected from it. Most vitally for me, the neuronormativity attached to the support I was accessing was contributing to an increase in my masking and a deterioration in my mental health, all of which culminated in me landing in my doctor's surgery, telling a stranger that I wanted to die.

2. Being a parent in a Neurodivergent household is stressful AF

There has been significant research into the impact of caring for a disabled child. It is well documented that caring for a disabled child can – and does – have an impact on parental mental health. Research from Sweden in 2001 found that mothers of

Autistic children had elevated depression scores, with 50% of female parents showing signs of depression, compared to 15-21% in the other groups. In the same research, single mothers of children with disabilities were found to be more vulnerable to severe depression than mothers living with a partner.

In my work supporting parents and carers of Neurodivergent children, the thing I see more than anything else is the overwhelming pressure these parents are under – the battle to secure basic support; the neverending ableism; the worry that comes with seeing how the world treats Neurodivergent folks; the extra energy, patience, compassion and sheer hard work that comes with advocating for a Neurodivergent child or young person. It all places an incredible strain on us as caregivers.

I am not a fan of wearing our children's challenges as a badge of honour. I certainly don't want us to go down the route of adding to the disenfranchisement of our children and young people by the "othering" of them. I also see the damage that's done when parents don't feel able to be honest about how hard they are finding things. In my attempt to protect him, I did all I could to ensure that people didn't look at my child as a burden. It was a noble goal and I think one many parents can relate to but ultimately, it left me deep in overwhelm with no way out. I had to be the strong one, the reliable one, the articulate one. I became the parent who could make a case for support for their child without getting too emotional. In advocating for my child, I had to be highly skilled at masking my struggles. The cost of that was high. Almost too high. I paid with my mental health and almost with my life.

3. Life expectancy for Autistic people is significantly reduced by our increased risk of suicide

Research from the University of Cambridge has shown that up to 66% of Autistic adults have thought about taking their own life, and 35% have attempted suicide. Around 1% of people in the UK are diagnosed as Autistic, yet "up to 15% of people hospitalised after attempting suicide have a diagnosis of autism".

Research has also found that both diagnosed Autistic people and those "with elevated Autistic traits" are more vulnerable to mental health problems, suicidal thoughts and behaviours. Cambridge

University Research from 2014 also showed that:

> "Autistic people on average die 20 years earlier than non-Autistic people, and two big causes of this are suicide and epilepsy."

Writing me a prescription for the antidepressants I had stopped taking six months previously (yes, I know!) Dr. Bolder went on to call me every day (apart from Christmas Day) for the next two weeks. She had me come into the surgery twice more. I didn't realise it at the time but that doctor was doing what I couldn't do for myself at that moment – she was giving me tiny goals to keep me alive whilst I was deep in Autistic Burnout. She was saving my life.

* * *

Please know

Regardless of your neurotype, being a parent is HARD. What's more, being a parent in a Neurodivergent household is extra hard. It doesn't make you a shitty human or a rubbish parent to admit that.

Poor mental health is in no way a moral failing.

Contrary to popular belief, if someone is feeling suicidal, talking about it and being asked gentle questions will reduce, not increase, the chances of a person acting on those feelings. If you are experiencing suicidal thoughts or feelings, you deserve to have someone listen to you and to be supported as you navigate your way through what I know can feel utterly overwhelming.

8

Trauma and Stress Responses

A Whistlestop Tour of Polyvagal Theory

When I was thirteen, my mum came home from my Parents' Evening with a perplexed look on her face. As usual, it had been a glowing report. As usual, I could see that my Mum was genuinely puzzled.

"Well, I don't know who is going to school and pretending to be you because the child they described sounds like an absolute dream," she exclaimed, as she threw her coat off and slumped into a chair.

Looking back on it, I can see why she was confused. On the surface, I was a polite, compliant, people pleaser but underneath, it felt like I was sitting on a burning ball of big feelings that threatened to erupt at any moment. Earlier in my childhood, those feelings did erupt sometimes, much to the surprise of those around me. Aged seven, I smacked the kid from next door round the head with a spade because they put sand in my Dad's cement mixer, and we weren't allowed to do that. At nine, I stabbed a boy in my class in the arm with a pair of scissors because he pulled a chair out from underneath me. I regularly had what my Mum called "flip outs" when I threw things around, shouted and screamed, packed a bag, and threatened to leave home.

Over time, I worked out how to keep a lid on the volcano when outside our home. At school, I was a Grade A student who never stepped out of line but when I got home, the lid would come off and I was a loud, abrasive, headstrong teenager with a defiant streak and a potty mouth. I was the perfect example of the now commonly-recognised "coke bottle effect" kid.

Of course, I didn't understand any of that at the time. I didn't know that I was masking in school. It wasn't conscious. I would have meltdowns almost every day after school and it made me feel terrible. When my mum told me after parents' evening that she wished I could be as good at home as I was at school, I wanted to tell her that I hated school. I wanted to tell her that I was desperately lonely. That I felt like an alien. That I thought I was broken. That my big feelings frightened me.

I couldn't find the words to say any of that so, instead, I screamed in her face:

"You don't fucking understand!"

I stormed upstairs, slammed my bedroom door, and threw myself on my bed in a fit of frustrated, frightened tears.

* * *

What I didn't know then

1. Lashing out, running away, and masking are all subconscious survival responses.

Kate Jones is a Psychotherapist, a very wise person, and Chief Communications Officer at Neuroclastic. She's also one of my closest friends. Kate has helped me to understand a lot more about my experience as an undiagnosed Neurodivergent child. One of the game-changing things I have learned from Kate is Polyvagal Theory.

My layman's explanation of Polyvagal Theory

Introduced in 1994 by Stephen Porges, the simple basics of Polyvagal Theory is that survival (actual, emotional, and mental) requires us to be in a place where we are safe to make connections with other people as our authentic selves. Polyvagal calls this our ventral vagus or "Safe and Social" state. When we are not in a Safe and Social state this is because a primal, involuntary stress response, managed by the vagus nerve, has set off an "internal fire alarm" to let us know that we are in danger.

Our vagus nerve acts as a messenger, picking up on stimuli from our environment,

which can trigger a stress response. Our
central nervous system is constantly
scanning our environment and sending
signals to our brain, via the vagus nerve. If
we sense a threat (no matter how small)
that places us outside our Safe and Social
state, our brain will trigger one of three
sympathetic nervous system responses.

The three sympathetic nervous system
responses are:

1. Fight

When triggered by our vagus nerve fire
alarm, our brain asks "Can I protect myself
by being assertive and facing the threat
head-on?" If the answer to this is yes, we
will respond in "Fight" mode. When in a
Fight response we may feel angry or tense;
we might become defensive in our
interactions; we may be verbally or

physically aggressive, and it may trigger an explosion of big feelings.

I remember one occasion at university, after a night clubbing, my Fight response was triggered by a seemingly small incident. As the nightclub was clearing and the lights came on, I lost my friends in the crush of people. I was immediately thrown into a full-blown Fight response. I was gripped by rage, screaming and lashing out at anyone who tried to calm me down. My anger volcano erupted as I flailed my arms in a blind panic. I punched a bouncer as they tried to remove me from the club and the police were called.

The worst bit about that experience was not the distress I felt at finding myself alone in a nightclub (although that was really unpleasant). It wasn't even being told off by a Police Officer (again, not fun).

What was hardest for me was the way that my friends behaved and spoke about what had happened, afterwards. They made jokes and teased me. It was clear that the incident changed the way they viewed me. I learned from that experience that it wasn't safe for me to be in Fight response and not just because I risked being arrested. I learned that my "big feelings" meant that people around me treated me differently and that felt like an even bigger danger.

2. Flight

When our stress response is triggered and fighting isn't an option for whatever reason, the next question our brain asks is "Can I protect myself by moving away from the threat?"

This was what happened to me every time I packed a bag to leave home. It's what happens when children are "runners", which can be terrifying for all involved. I know a good number of families whose Neurodivergent children experience intense Flight responses, including kids who run away from their parents in public places, go missing from their own homes, and abscond from school. As well as making an actual run for it, the Flight response can also show up as another means of avoiding the threat. That can include substance use and addiction, becoming physically agitated or being unable to sit still, and avoiding situations or people. If Fight isn't safe but Flight is, that may result in us becoming withdrawn over time as we make attempts to avoid triggers in our environment.

3. Fawn
Fawn is the place where many Neurodivergent people land most often.

When Fight and Flight just aren't cutting it, our brain asks "Can I protect myself by rejecting or suppressing my true self?" This is where masking comes in but Fawn can also show up as people-pleasing or compulsive helpfulness, over-apologising even when things aren't our fault, pretending to be ok when we aren't, and saying yes to things we don't want to.

It's important to understand that Fight, Flight, and Fawn responses are not choices. It's also helpful to understand that over time, those well-trodden neural pathways mean our bodies and brains might come to "favour" a particular response because it's the one that works best most often. That's why some Neurodivergent people have an (unfair) reputation for overreacting (Fight response). It's why some Neurodivergent kids are known to be "runners" (Flight response). And it's why so many of us spent years masking (Fawn). All three responses are automatic, happening in a split second and without conscious thought. All three come with feelings of anxiety, confusion, and frustration as we ask ourselves "Why am I like this?" Learning how to recognise these responses in ourselves and our children helps us to be more understanding of the dynamics at play in our homes.

2. Triggers and stressors are different for everyone

Our Polyvagal responses are shaped and influenced not only by our neurotype but also by our experiences. Learning about polyvagal gave me the ability to understand why I respond in the way I do. It gave me permission to acknowledge that I have big feelings a lot of the time and that rather than being an indication that I am "broken", it's evidence that I am human. It also helped me to understand that, for all that my child is similar to me, his stress and trauma responses are quite different.

Theo's mask fell away when he was 14, never to go back on. His experience saw him step into the state at the opposite end of the scale to Safe and Social when Fawn stopped being effective. Theo spent several months in shutdown, unable to leave the house. He experienced periods of situational mutism when he was unable to communicate verbally. Polyvagal theory calls this the Dorsal Vagus or "Freeze" state. It's where many Neurodivergent people find themselves after an extended period of Masking or Fawn.

One of the indicators that Theo was making a recovery from burnout was when he lost his temper and shouted at a friend. Whilst other people around us were a bit taken aback at my son's seemingly sudden outburst, I rejoiced in it. Not because I like a scrap, but because I knew that it meant Theo was out of Freeze state and back into being able to respond naturally to his internal fire alarm. He and his friend patched things up very quickly and Theo learned in that moment that it was safe for him to assert himself when he felt under threat.

3. "If it was safe to be yourself, you would be"

We know that Neurodivergent neurology means that Neurodivergent people experience the world differently to neurotypical folks. We experience emotions differently and with different intensities. We experience our senses differently and our life experiences are coloured by that. As a result, our polyvagal responses can be bigger, more often, more intense, and more disabling than those experienced by neurotypical people. Once we know this, it opens the door for us to be much kinder to ourselves and the people around us.

Somewhere around the age of 10, I started lying. It started as small fibs but quickly snowballed to the point that I lied about anything and everything. I'd lie to my friends about what I had done at the weekend. I would lie to my parents about what had happened in school. I lied about starting my period. I lied about where I was going, what I was doing, and with whom. When I was 11, I even lied about being able to see when I pretended to have lost my sight after I bumped my head at a family fun day. It was only when an ambulance was called that my sight was miraculously restored.

I didn't know why I was lying but I knew I couldn't stop. It lasted for around two years and it's something that bothered me for a long time after the lies ended. When I heard Kate Jones say about masking "If it was safe to be yourself, you would be" I felt a huge amount of relief. I realised that the lies were from a time in my life when I was so deep in Fawn response that it wasn't safe for me to tell the truth about even the smallest thing. Understanding that the compulsion to lie was part of my Fawn response, took some of the shame away.

* * *

Please know

When a person is in stress response, they are not "choosing" their responses consciously.

Understanding trauma, stress responses, and triggers for everyone in a Neurodivergent household can help us to be kinder to ourselves and more compassionate with others.

If you have been someone who has felt ashamed of your big feelings or your Fight, Flight, or Fawn responses, it's time to cut yourself some slack.

Regardless of what someone's triggers are or how their responses present themselves, everyone deserves to feel safe, including you.

147

9

Community

The Antidote to Loneliness

Loneliness is a common experience for parents of Neurodivergent children and young people. When you have a child who struggles with things other kids their age enjoy, you can feel incredibly isolated. Being around other parents is especially tricky. For me, that goes back as far as the primary school gate chats that I didn't feel a part of. The chasm between our family and others really opened up when Theo hit his teen years. I recall one particular conversation I had when I went on a speed awareness course (don't judge me, I have

ADHD and I drive too fast when I am late for things, which is all the fucking time!). During a coffee break I ended up next to a very glamorous-looking Sales Rep. I don't remember her name but she was wearing a jumpsuit.

Jumpsuit Jenny: "Have you got kids, hun?"

Me: "Yes. A son. He's 15."

Jump-the-lights Jenny: "God. I bet he's a handful. Is he into cars and girls and all that?"

Me: "Not really. Lego is his thing."

Judgy Jenny: "My son liked lego when he was younger. He's 14. Too old for all that now, obviously. What school does he go to?"

Me: "He doesn't go to school at the moment. He's not been well."

Just-so-nosey Jenny: "Oh. I see. What's wrong with him?"

Me, starting to wish I had gone outside with my coffee: "Erm. He has really bad anxiety. He's waiting to be assessed for autism."

Jump-to-conclusions Jenny: "Oh, God Bless him." She gives me the sympathetic head-tip-to-one-side that I have come to know well. "My sister's next-door neighbour's milkman's son has autism. He is very severe. He eats soap and bangs his head on the floor in Tescos. I don't know how you do it, babes."

Me: "Well, every Autistic person is different. For example, my son —"

Jumping-out-of-the-conversation Jenny:
"Anyway, you keep your chin up, hun.
You're so brave."

And off she skips across the room to find
another Speedy Gonzales to chat to, no
doubt hoping the next one is better at
small talk than I turned out to be.

* * *

There is a sense of dread that comes
over me when I know that something is
heading my way that will "out" my child
as different. Sometimes I see them coming:
Sports days, prize-giving ceremonies,
parties, sleepovers, exams, day trips,
holidays, airports, weddings, fireworks
displays, restaurants, public bathrooms,
buffets . . . all a potential minefield of too
many variables for Neurodivergent people.

Other times it will be an out-of-the-blue conversation like the one I had with Just-Fuck-Off Jenny.

Conversations like that happen fairly regularly nowadays and I feel better prepared. Early on in our journey, they would leave me feeling that I had let my son down. I felt a burden of responsibility to explain to the other person that he was different, but not less. That in our house, being Autistic wasn't seen as a deficit. I had feelings of guilt at not having been able to use the opportunity to educate someone about neurodivergence. The more conversations I had with people who didn't have shared experiences, the more isolated and alone I felt.

What I didn't know then

1. The Jennys are everywhere!

Being around people who just don't get it, can be exhaustingly isolating and incredibly painful. Out in the wild, there are folks like Just-fuck-off Jenny at every turn, making it harder to fearlessly show up for yourself and your child. There is no quicker route to feeling like you are losing your marbles than being around people who don't have the first idea about what it's like to be a parent in a Neurodivergent household. Jennies come with a full set of stereotypes and ableist assumptions, hardwired. Until they want – or need – to do the work required to see things differently, it's unlikely they will. Whilst their careless words and throwaway comments do not usually come with malicious intentions, it's important that we acknowledge how damaging they can be.

2. You have choices

Initially, when faced with a Jenny, I would feel that I should try to use every opportunity to help them unpick some of their inaccurate misconceptions. Thing is, that takes a lot of energy, and whilst – on occasion – I was able to have meaningful conversations where I felt like I had helped someone move the dial on their misunderstandings, I exhausted myself in the process. Over time I came to understand that there was no shame in deciding to not engage in those conversations that tired me and hurt me. I was allowed to sidestep those difficult interactions if that was in my best interest. If, in order to take care of my tired body and overwhelmed brain, I needed to disengage and just nod along on occasion, that was ok. Just because my mask was off,

154

it didn't mean I wasn't allowed to pop it back on (albeit wonkily) when necessary, in the interest of self-care and as an act of self-compassion.

I found that in having conversations with lots of people about what we were experiencing, I felt an extra burden. It made me feel more alone and isolated and less supported and understood. Sometimes it brought unnecessary pain and suffering to my door. Once I made the decision to be more discerning in who I shared things with and when, I felt like I gave myself permission to prioritise my own mental health and save my energy for the times I really needed it. When I was deep in Fight response, trying to advocate for my child, it was so easy to lose sight of those choices and give myself permission to make them.

3. There ARE people who will understand

One of the main reasons for writing this
book was so that I could let other parents
know that they are not alone. For a
long time, I thought our family was the
only family experiencing life as we were.
Interactions like the one I had with Just-
ignorant Jenny were commonplace. However,
once I discovered that there were (mainly
online) spaces where parents like me
were sharing their experiences, supporting
one another, and having the conversations
I desperately needed to have, it was like
a whole new world opened up to me.

For me, finding an online community of
kindred souls was like finding a door to a
secret garden. But rather than being
populated with wildflowers and luscious
plants, this garden was rich with

neurodivergence-affirming parents who were determined to see their children as individuals, not stereotypes. The garden was a glorious maze of self-discovery where I found a community of like-minded parents who – like me – swung between stumbling about in the shrubbery of self-doubt to skipping through fields of validation.

What we all had in common was a heartfelt commitment to doing the work required to see and support our children as individuals. Together we challenged our preconceptions about neurodivergence. Collectively we pushed back and rebelled against those ableist stereotypes that had stood between us and the truth that our children were gloriously Neurodivergent.

I am much more comfortable in online spaces than in face-to-face environments so initially, I joined multiple Facebook groups in a bid to find a place I felt at "home". Some groups were not for me. Others very quickly felt like a pair of very comfy slippers. A place to be me without fear of judgment. Some of the people I have connected with in those spaces have become dear and trusted friends. They are the people I have come to know I can rely on when times are especially tough.

* * *

Please know

Finding your "people" can be life-affirming, life-changing, and life-saving. Having people at the other end of a Facebook message, cut through the loneliness that had overwhelmed me for most of my adult life.

You are allowed to decide who you listen to, who you give time to, and who you let take up space in your brain.

Finding the right Community can take a bit of trial and error: not all spaces are created equal and it's ok to "shop around" until you find a place that fits you.

You deserve to have people in your life who will hold space for you to show up as your authentic, messy, sad, lonely, confused, overwhelmed self.

10

Final Thoughts

Permission to Become THAT Parent

I have learned that it's not enough to "know" about sensory differences and social anxiety; masking and burnout; behaviour modification and trust; stereotypes, ableism, gaslighting and consent; diagnosis and labels; hereditary neurodivergence and mental health; trauma and stress responses. Knowledge is power. Knowing what to do with that power is where the magic happens.

You have the opportunity to put into action all you know. To step up and push back. To decide to parent with radical acceptance. To be *that* parent. I won't lie to you: it's not always going to be easy. What I've learned is that when you prioritise your relationship with your child and your own mental health, you WILL be met with resistance. When that happens you WILL question yourself. You'll have days, weeks, and months when you feel like you are wading through treacle. There will be times when you fuck up. You'll be angry, sad, frustrated, and overwhelmed on occasion. You will be told you are unreasonable, unrealistic, emotional, and irrational. Your decisions will be challenged and questioned. People will judge you. Some days you'll feel pushed to your limits.

And it will be worth it.

Being *that* parent means being the parent your child needs you to be. It means protecting your relationship with them and putting their trust in you above the opinions of others. It means showing them they matter. It means doing things your own way. It means trusting your gut. It means practising self-compassion and that takes . . . well . . . practice.

* * *

Whilst you are finding your feet with your route to becoming that parent, you can make things a little easier on yourself in the here and now. You can give yourself permission to be and do some of the things you might previously have denied yourself. I suggest making a list. You can use mine if you like.

You are allowed.

You are allowed to be 'that' parent.

Your Child is Not Broken

You are allowed to get things wrong.

You are allowed to be tired.

You are allowed to have big feelings.

You are allowed to do things the way that works best for you and your family.

You are allowed to take your time.

You are allowed to say No.

You are allowed to build a blanket fort.

You are allowed to eat ice cream for breakfast and stay in your PJs all day.

You are allowed to ditch the idea that things have to be a particular way.

You are allowed to need some things to be just so.

You are allowed to experiment with finding out what works best for your family.

You are allowed to decide whose advice you take, and whose you ignore.

You are allowed to step away from people and situations where you don't feel safe.

You are allowed to ignore the washing up.

You are allowed to sit on the floor at the airport.

You are allowed to swing on your chair.

You are allowed to take your shoes off in public.

You are allowed to dance in the supermarket.

You are allowed to arrive late and leave early.

You are allowed to ask for help.

You are allowed to not know all the answers.

You are allowed to feel frustrated.

You are allowed to be unsure.

You are allowed to cry.

You are allowed to laugh.

You are allowed to sit in the car as long as you need to.

You are allowed to sing in the shower.

You are allowed to dance in your kitchen.

You are allowed to bounce on the bed.

You are allowed to be upside-down.

You are allowed to play with blu-tac.

You are allowed to make a mess.

You are allowed to say fuck, bugger, arse, and c*nt.

You are allowed to add things to this list.

* * *

Whatever permissions you give yourself, I want to thank you for being open to doing things differently. We need more parents like you, who will courageously lead by example. We need parents who push back against stereotypes, challenge ableism, and who are committed to raising a generation of self-assured Neurodivergent adults. We need parents like you who look at their own children and know that they are not broken.

Congratulations on being *that* parent.

I'm glad you're here.

Photo © Nelly Naylor

Afterword: What the Fig?

April 2023, Yorkshire

Well, bugger me! Tie me to the railings and call me Suzy if my little book didn't go down a lot better than I expected. Here I am, sitting at my desk in our spare room, squeezed between the spare bed that doubles as a shelf for unfiled paperwork and a large stack of empty cardboard boxes. My Publisher has suggested I write a little something, to sum up what's happened in the last few months. It's been quite a ride.

The week before I released *Your Child Is Not Broken* in January 2023, my friend

Lindsay said to me "I have a feeling this book is going to change lives." I laughed it off. Lindsay, like most of my close friends, knows me well enough to know that my ego needs a good ole rub from time to time. Like many other late-identified Autistic people, I often find myself taken hostage by my incessant need for validation. I don't know if it's down to the years of masking and people-pleasing, my over-active imagination, my trauma profile, the fact that I feel like I can FINALLY ask for what I need, or just my Rejection Sensitive Dysphoria (more on that in a bit). Maybe it's all of those things. So when Lindsay said she could feel it in her delightfully Yorkshire bones that the book was going to do well, I put it down to her just being a really good pal who knows that my love language is Words of Affirmation.

Regardless of the root cause, it seems my inner imposter (his name is Nigel) upped his game as the release date hurtled toward me. The manuscript had been signed off months before and I had thought I was happy with it but as the publication date approached, Nigel launched a campaign to convince me that every word I had written was complete and utter shite. Nigel regularly locks me in a dark room of self-doubt, especially at times when things seem to be going quite well. Just as I am relaxing into the comfort of my new-found confidence, Nigel grabs me by the chin and screams in my face "nobody likes you!" Nigel REALLY enjoyed the run-up to the book being released.

I set an alarm early on release day to check the Amazon charts (something that would become more than a mild compulsion in the following weeks). I remember being mildly amused that my book was in the "New Releases" chart just below "Pooping Dogs Calendar". Yep. A calendar of photos of dogs taking a shit was outselling me, keeping me in my place, reminding me not to get too excited about the fact I had written a real-life book that real-life people could order. Nigel loved that!

What happened next was a bit of a head fuck. My friend Linsday was right. It turns out this book is not just the book I needed to write; it's also the book thousands of parents and carers needed to read. From the day *Your Child Is Not Broken* went on sale, my email and social media inboxes lit up like a Christmas tree. I very quickly lost track of all the messages from other families, telling me that our experiences mirrored theirs. I wasn't able to keep up with notifications on Facebook from people tagging me in testimonials. Within days of release, my little book sprinted up the Amazon charts, barging past the shitting dogs, elbowing Davina McCall out of the way, and climbing to number four on the whole of Amazon. The same week, I was approached by three different publishers who wanted to buy the global rights. The following week we hit number nine in the *Sunday Times* Bestsellers list. I lost my shit for a bit. It was all quite overwhelming.

Nigel upped his game. He spent the next few days whispering "you are such a fucking wanker" in my ear as a reminder to not get too big for my boots. He made sure that the occasional not-so-great review on Amazon was imprinted in my brain. He gave me a cruel nudge in the ribs when a handful of people said that they hated the title. His side-eye was strong when some folks pulled me up on my writing style, claiming it was "patronising", "teenager-ish" and "unnecessarily sweary". Nigel stuck the review that questioned whether I was actually Autistic on the fridge in my brain. Because Nigel is a right twat.

I was reminded by those close to me that "everyone is entitled to an opinion". A dear friend told me "Just like bum holes – everyone has an opinion. Doesn't mean you have to look at them." So, I printed out my favourite Dita Von Teese quote and stuck it over Nigel's offering on the door of my brain fridge:

"You can be the ripest, juiciest peach in the world and there's still going to be someone who hates peaches."

Fuck you, Nigel!

And here's the thing . . .

It **DOES** make me feel like a bit of a wanker to say that I am a *Sunday Times* Bestseller. No matter how much I agree with Dita, it **DOES** bother me that some people don't like my book. It **DOES** hurt that people have dismissed and invalidated my and Theo's experiences. Because RSD is an absolute bugger.

I didn't touch on RSD much in the first edition of the book, but given it has been so prevalent for me in recent months and given that I have this opportunity to add more value, I thought I'd unpick it a little here in the hope it might help other Neurodivergent folks in understanding themselves. Because – as it turns out – it doesn't matter that you have over 300 five-star reviews on Amazon, those couple of people who didn't like the book, really did kick me in the self-esteem. I know that's RSD doing its thing.

RSD in layman's terms

Rejection Sensitive Dysphoria (RSD) is described by neuroclastic.com as a common issue for Neurodivergent people whereby we experience "a heightened sensitivity to real, perceived, or anticipated rejection." It is thought that RSD is particularly debilitating for Neurodivergent people because it is underpinned by an increased difficulty in regulating our emotions, which leads to an incredibly heightened response to any and all kinds of rejection.

RSD and me

As I've come to understand myself more, I've come to understand just how prevalent a role RSD has played in my life. The genuine belief growing up that I was "different" from other people (not in a good way), coupled with my desperate need to be liked, accepted and understood as a child, young person and adult have hardwired the fear of rejection or being "found out" into the deepest parts of my being. It's the crippling fear of rejection that meant my "mask" was so intact for so many years. It's probably why I will never be able to fully unmask. And it's why I am STILL so frigging sensitive to criticism which – as it turns out – is quite tricky when you write a book about your life experiences and put it out into the world.

What I didn't realise until very recently was that the masks I created to protect myself from RSD, to stop people from discovering the "real me", actually exposed me to greater hurt. The constant quest for eye contact; the exhausting battle to stop me from interrupting conversations; the self-imposed silence that came from knowing that if I spoke my mind people might turn on me; the people-pleasing . . . all made me MORE susceptible to RSD. Because they all moved me further away from being able to "be myself" and learn to like myself. That – in turn – meant that when I felt attacked, I didn't have the sense of self-worth I needed to rise above it.

There is nothing more impossible to do as a person gripped by RSD than to "just ignore it". For so many years, RSD has had me wrapped in a cycle of fear of people seeing the "real" me and hating what they saw. In my twenties, this fear often swung to shame in the knowledge that I wasn't "being myself". And the cycle kept feeding itself, keeping me away from connecting to my core sense of who I am. I was stripped of the ability to "shake it off" because my masks meant I didn't have the chance to prove to myself that I wasn't a useless human. Yes, Taylor Swift, the haters ARE gonna hate hate hate hate but you make it sound a lot bloody easier than it actually is to shake it off.

Please know

Rejection Sensitivity Dysphoria shows up for different people in different ways. For many of us, it's something that pulls us into a cycle of self-criticism without us even realising what's happening. RSD is also cumulative – so the longer and harder you have been masking, and the more fuckery you've been faced with, the more intense your RSD will be. It might be that your RSD shows up as avoiding asking for feedback or

– at the other extreme – always asking for reassurance. Maybe it throws you into a fight response over what appears to be the tiniest thing. Often it will tie itself to particular trigger words or phrases to give those feelings of pure panic extra oomph.

Whatever RSD does to you, it's useful to remind yourself that just because something isn't a big deal to anyone else, that doesn't mean it can't be a big deal to you. RSD is the bedfellow of trauma. As a parent in a Neurodivergent household, RSD will most likely be triggered more regularly in your dealings with professionals than it might be for other parents. That doesn't make you "wrong". It doesn't mean that you are oversensitive, dramatic, silly, unnecessary or inappropriate. It definitely doesn't mean you are a rubbish human.

The antidote to RSD

There's some excellent work on RSD on the neuroclastic.com website. I'd encourage you to go and read "On Rejection Sensitive Dysphoria, Codependency, and Identity: How to get out from behind the masks" by Terra Vance. What that article picks out is that unmasking and reconnecting to your core self are the first steps to finding a way to manage your RSD. There are some really useful tips on how to start doing that.

Learning to live with RSD is a work in progress. One of the first things I did as part of my unmasking was to embrace my potty mouth. If you think this book is sweary, you should hear the absolute filth inside my head. Keeping all that in for over 40 years has been exhausting. So, when people criticised my sweary writing style, my

RSD had a motherfucking field day. Nigel reminded me that I was "inappropriate", "vulgar" and "unlikeable" and told me that my dirty mouth was probably going to end my career as an author. I spiralled into a pit of self-loathing. Yes, RSD is an absolute git face.

I'm not a peach

All this got me thinking . . . what if I'm not a juicy peach after all? What if trying to tell myself I am is just another mask? Maybe I'm more of a furry fig. Figs aren't as universally appealing. Not as palatable or as squeezable or as easy on the eye or the stomach. Sometimes figs are sweet; sometimes a bit bitter. Figs are robust as fuck. Figs are known for having pretty aggressive root systems: strangler figs grow their roots down from the tops of their host trees ultimately killing and replacing them. I like that. I think I'm a fig. Embracing my figginess is making it easier to give myself permission to remain visible; to keep sharing our story in its imperfect, not-very-peachy state.

When I accepted the offer from Bluebird to republish the book, I decided that the main body would remain pretty much unchanged from the first edition. That's intentional. Because what the hundreds of messages I received from people who DID relate to the book told me that this little book is doing what it's meant to, for the people it's meant to. The figs get it.

I have had messages from people whose lightbulb moments from our story included realising they needed to seek mental health support; who finally felt like they understood Autistic overwhelm in their children; who felt braver about withdrawing consent for the use of violent restraint against their young people in school; who had "a-ha" moments about their own neurotype; who had also been told to "touch the gate" (so many people have been told to touch the gate); who felt empowered to trust their gut; who felt validated, seen, heard, no longer alone. Quite a lot of people laughed. A lot of folks cried. One person has told me that reading the chapter about feeling suicidal meant they didn't make the attempt to unalive themself that they had been planning.

So, there we are. Some musings on life as a Bestselling Author (or "utter wanker" as Nigel prefers to call me). This is a book by a fig who is working on their RSD to give fewer figs in the future. It's written for other figs who deserve to figging flourish. In the spirit of that, I have pulled together some extra content for this second edition of the book. Some extra "figgy" content. Some research. Some fun stuff. A lovely poem. Think of it as a "here's some extra stuff in no particular order that I found value in and I think you might too."

I hope you figging like it.

Heidi

From the Horse's Mouth: What Does Theo Have to Say About All This?

Since releasing the book, lots of people have asked me about Theo. People want to know what happened after we decided to stop touching the gate. The long-story-short is that Theo is in recovery from his burnout and in September 2022 he started an animal management course in a mainstream college, which has been the making of him.

Theo is living proof that recovery and a return to education after burnout and mental health crisis ARE possible. It's certainly not been plain sailing and we have had to do a lot of work and liaising with his college AND Theo is thriving in a mainstream college now that we know how to support him. Theo had two years of no school and missed all of his GCSE syllabus. He was deep in burnout and mental health crisis and it was pretty bleak for a while. We turned a corner when we were able to get him a place in a specialist Pupil Referral Unit (PRU) for students with mental health needs. After Theo left the PRU he had a 12-month programme of home-based, bespoke education, with support from a Neurodivergent-affirming occupational therapist, tutors and mentors. Slowly, his confidence was reinstated. Gradually, his self-esteem was rebuilt. He developed the self-advocacy skills needed to be able to return to education.

When writing the book, I was conscious that it didn't capture the voices of children and young people, so when I had the opportunity to add some new content, I asked Theo if I could interview him. What follows is an abridged transcript of that conversation. Theo didn't want to speak about the trauma he experienced in school (he still finds it incredibly distressing to do so) so, instead, we spoke about what has happened since we abandoned Operation Touchgate and his advice for other families experiencing what we did.

It's a Thursday evening. We are sitting side by side on the sofa. Theo is playing Sims while we chat.

Me: "So, when did you first realise that things were going to get better?"

Theo: "When I was at the PRU . . . I just felt a bit happier there. It was a good place and they understood me . . . It was nice and it was smaller. I had friends there . . . They weren't shouting. I didn't have to wear a uniform. I had friends."

Me: "And what do you remember about those first days at the PRU?"

Theo: "You've got a proper interview voice you, haven't you?" [Theo chuckles] "On my second day at the PRU the headteacher got punched in the face. Hit in the side of the face by this kid who was bigger than he was. But it was good. They were nice. It was smaller. We called teachers by their first names. There was a lot less pressure. Just less pressure in general. No one forced you to do anything you didn't want to do. There was a chillout room with a really comfy leather sofa. It was an old conservatory out the back of the building."

Me: "So what was the best bit about the PRU?"

Theo: "Meeting new people. I felt like I had missed out on things when I wasn't in school. Just things everyone else was doing. After the PRU when we couldn't find a placement that was a bit stressful. The Local Authority wanted me to go to the local college and I didn't want to go in there. When I finally got a place in a college I wanted to go to that was quite stressful too. They all seemed a little bit unprepared. I remember you had to send a lot of emails."

Me: "So, what's made the difference in college? How has that stress been manageable?"

Theo: "My course manager. She's nice. She's read my EHCP."

Me: "What does she do for you that you feel the teachers at your old school didn't do for you?"

Theo: "I dunno. It's kind of a different attitude at college. The same as at the PRU. You're not a child."

Me: "What about when exams came around?"

Theo: "Yeah that was stressful again, wasn't it? You shouted at them and got it sorted. I worried a little bit it wouldn't get sorted. But you told me it would so that was OK."

Me: "So do you believe me when I say things are going to get sorted?"

Theo: "Now I do, yeah."

Me: "But you didn't used to?"

Theo: "No."

Me: "Why not?"

Theo: "Because sometimes it didn't get sorted and things took ages to get done."

Me: "But you believe me now? You trust me?"

Theo: "Mostly, yes."

Me: "Mostly?"

Theo: "I wouldn't trust you to pull me from a burning building but . . ."

Me: "You wouldn't trust me to pull you from a burning building?!"

Theo: "Mum. You can't even walk down the stairs without falling over."

[I laugh and an audible fart slips out]

Theo: "I expect you to put the fart noise into the transcript of this conversation, Mum."

Me: "Noted. So, if you could go back and speak to yourself when it all went belly up, what would you tell yourself?"

Theo: "That it would be alright. And I'd say get your Mum to get you into that PRU sooner. We could have done that."

Me: "What do you think that parents need to know?"

Theo: "I don't know. That's why you wrote your book, isn't it?"

Me: "If you had a time machine . . ."

Theo: "I don't have a time machine. These kind of questions don't work with my brain."

Me: "OK. What do you wish that I'd known?"

Theo: "That I was Autistic."

Me: "Do you think that would have made a difference?"

Theo: "If you'd known earlier? Yeah . . . It would have been better. It would have been easier. Because maybe we would have got support sorted a bit sooner. If you look at my nursery records I think it's pretty obvious."

Me: "What do you think I missed?"

Theo: "I don't think you missed it. I think other people missed it." [A beat.] "Why? What would you look for now?"

Me: "Erm. Difficulties with friendships. Big feelings. Stimming. Intense interests. Quirkiness."

Theo: "Yeah. All that. Good answer."

[See how he tricked me here?]

Me: "I'm supposed to one the one asking questions, Theo." [He grins at me.] "So what do you think needs to change in mainstream schools for them to be autism friendly?"

Theo: "Mainstream Schools. They just need to change in general. They're not built for anybody. To be fair, I don't think anybody gets on OK in mainstream."

Me: "Do you not?"

Theo: "No."

Me: "Not anyone?"

Theo: "Well . . . like . . . Even if you look at the kids who look like they are doing OK in mainstream . . . everyone is just a bit insecure, aren't they?"

Me: "Even neurotypical kids?"

Theo: "Yeah. Pretty much. I don't know very many neurotypical people. I stay away from them."

Me: "Tell me what the perfect school would be like. If you could open your own school."

Theo: "Small. Higher teacher-to-student ratio. Lots of teaching assistants."

Me: "Small in terms of the size of the building or . . ."

Theo: "Both. Small building. Fewer kids. Big sports field. Big art department."

Me: "And what would you require of your teachers in your school?"

Theo: "Low arousal approach . . . And for them not to be knobheads."

Me: "Not be knobheads. Gotcha. What do you think was the most damaging thing for you in school?"

Theo: "I guess the whole attitude that because I was doing alright academically, it was OK."

Me: "And if you could wave a magic wand?"

Theo: "I don't have a magic wand, Mum. No time machine. No magic wand."

Me: "Sorry."

Theo: "Uniform. Get rid of blazers. I think there should still be a uniform like a polo shirt or whatever but blazers are fucking awful. They are sticky. Just awful. Sticky. And they absorb water."

Me: "What else?"

Theo: "Get rid of old-fashioned, shouty teachers who don't know what they are doing.

197

And stop putting newly qualified teachers on
their own in classrooms when they can't get
anyone to listen to them. I think the way
schools do stuff is a problem. It's the whole
discipline thing. Like . . . the outcome should
be related to the action, otherwise, what's the
point? Don't call it punishment for a start. You
smash a plate, you clear it up and you go and
get another plate out of the cupboard. That
makes sense. Detentions are bullshit. My
school did 30-minute detentions. By the time
you sat down you were out again. Pointless.
Accountability. Not punishments."

Me: "What do you think the worst thing
about EHCPs is?"

Theo: "No one reads them."

[At this point we are interrupted by the dog
who appears with a stuffed toy in his

mouth, looking to play. A conversation follows where we can't remember where the stuffed toy came from. It's a fluffy squirrel. We have a giggle about the fact we got distracted by an actual squirrel and how we are, at that moment, an ADHD stereotype.]

Me: "What would you do if you had kids and they said they didn't want to go to school?"

Theo: "I wouldn't make them. I just wouldn't send them. If someone's kid says 'I don't want to go to school' they should say they don't have to."

Me: "What if they never ever go to school? Do you think school should be optional?"

Theo: "No. There needs to be education. There should be options though."

Me: "So, what do you say to people who say 'well, no kid wants to go to school'?"

Theo: "Well then . . . I'd say . . . if no kids want to go to school what's up with schools?"

[A long silence while I reflect on this kid's wisdom.]

Me: "What do you like most about being Autistic?"

Theo: "I think I have quite a creative imagination."

Me: "And the worst thing about being Autistic?"

Theo: "I don't think it's a bad thing. It's just the world around us isn't made for us. Isn't adapted enough."

Me: "Give me three pieces of advice for Autistic kids."

Theo: "I don't like 'give me advice' questions. Are you just going to keep trying to rephrase this question? This is like the Time Machine and the Magic Wand question."

Me: "OK. Sorry. What advice would you give to [name of Autistic child we know]'s Mum?"

Theo: "Not everything professionals say is correct. Sometimes it's the adults in the situation who need to change, rather than the child. And that just because your child isn't conventionally fitting in, it doesn't mean they are not going to fit in, anywhere, ever. It's not that they aren't going to do well if they aren't conventional or neurotypical. It might take a bit of adjustment but they should have access to things that everyone else has access to. And your child shouldn't be made to feel guilty for how they are acting if they can't help it."

Me: "And what would you want to say to the other kids around that child?"

Theo: "I don't know. I think the issue is that sometimes people don't talk about it because they are scared of saying the wrong thing. And actually having the conversation with the other children in the group so that they understand. People are too worried about saying something wrong. I would rather people were talking about it and acknowledging that there is a difference there but recognising that difference isn't a bad thing. You can teach that from a young age. This whole thing about Autistic kids having to be 'integrated' is bullshit. We shouldn't have to be integrated. If Autistic kids can be in mainstream and want to be then great. If not, we need better special schools. They shut them all to make us integrate. We still need special schools. I think integration is bullshit."

[I fart again, louder this time.]

Theo: "Bloody hell, Mother."

Me: "Sorry. What would you want to say to a parent who is being told by professionals to keep bringing their distressed kid into school?"

Theo: "If your child is getting distressed, don't do it. That would be my rule."

[He nods to indicate that he considers the conversation to be over.]

Me: "Thanks Theo."

Theo: "You're welcome."

[The dog puts the squirrel in Theo's lap.]

Photo © Vicki Head

School Refusal: A Mother's Experience of Parental Blame

By Megan Robertson

It starts as a small comment, fairly innocuous, with no indication of what it will become.

"Your child needs to push past their discomfort".

But they already do, you think, they don't want to be at home.

Home for them now is a lonely place.

Depressing.

They feel a failure.

Acutely aware they are getting further behind.

They want to go to school.

They can't, not won't.

In time, you notice a subtle, but significant change to the statement;

"You need to push them past their discomfort".

You are doing your best.

Your child is doing their best.

You know your child, but you ignore your own better judgement.

The pressure, the expectation and the shame all influence you.

Already past discomfort, you push them, repeatedly, into real fear and panic.

It doesn't help.

It never gets any easier.

In fact, it gradually gets worse.

The months go by.

Concerns are voiced about your own anxiety, and how this is impacting on your child.

It doesn't come from a place of compassion for you, but is another form of parental blame.

And you wonder, should they not be worried if you weren't anxious?

Given the devastatingly lonely and fearful life your child is now living?

Your child's mental health deteriorates.

Their mood is worryingly low.

OCD begins to take control of their life.

New professionals have become involved, with a specialist school now offered.

But the belief remains the same. With a little added extra:

"Your inability to witness your child feeling discomfort is stopping you from pushing them through it".

You try to explain what your child is actually experiencing.

They are way beyond mere discomfort, and regularly into terror.

If only the professionals could understand your reality.

Your voice is never heard.

It doesn't even dent the unwavering certainty and confidence in their belief.

Never doubting that this problem could be solved if only you pushed a little harder.

You puzzle over the origin of this, the conviction they all have that their theory is correct.

Despite a total absence of any evidence to support it.

You know only that it has been repeatedly written and never questioned.

With each additional entry into your child's notes, it becomes more established as "fact".

Meanwhile, the extreme anxiety which is preventing your child from fully engaging remains untreated.

The severity and underlying causes remain unrecognised, and unaddressed.

One day, the parent blame takes a new turn.

Your child has become unable to access any school provisions, struggling even with a "therapeutic" walk in the park.

There are a number of known factors contributing to this:

Severe anxiety.

School trauma.

Sensory overload.

Social difficulties.

Depression.

The list is not exhaustive, your child is complex.

You need an informed professional to see your child for the unique individual they are.

To plan a way forward.

You are desperate for a solution to help your child, for whom life has become simply intolerable.

Instead, a referral is made to social services.

The allegation shocks you to your core.

"We have been informed that you are placing barriers in the way of your child's education".

You are reeling from the betrayal of a school you initially believed had the expertise and understanding that your child needed.

Shaken, you try to make sense of this.

Disillusioned with the "specialist",
independent school, you realise your child's
inability to attend had three possible
causes:

Their needs are too great for this school.

The school is suitable, but failed to meet
their needs.

The mother is to blame.

The first two possibilities will impact on the
school's finances or reputation.

The third option was preferable.

The fear this elicits in you is instant and
overwhelming.

This is not a world you know, nor imagined
you ever would.

You have no experience of social workers,
your minimal knowledge gleaned only from
the news;

They remove children from their homes,
don't they?

The more rational part of you believes this
couldn't happen.

You've done nothing wrong after all.

Unable to be subdued is a deeper part,
feeling not thinking, and bringing with it a
primal fear.

You wake each morning with a sense of
dread.

Even your rational side has to recognise your new reality;

Professionals who do not understand your child have the power to make decisions about them.

So can you discount the worst-case scenario entirely?

That dread is always lurking just below the surface.

Finally the nightmare ends, with no explanation, no idea what was decided and why.

You are just happy it's over.

An all-consuming, horrendous episode in your life you can put behind you.

Except you can't.

In less than a year, you discover those damaging comments in the social worker's file will follow you.

They will influence the lens through which others perceive you.

You will be pre-judged, and uninformed opinions will again allow dubious decisions to be made about your child.

After months of living with an ever-worsening situation,

Reaching new, previously inconceivable lows,

Coping with life of torment for your child,

Who by now is barely able to leave their bedroom,

You will discover that another referral has been made.

This time by the CAMHS case worker, as they have not seen your child in six months.

It is seemingly irrelevant that they have barely visited in that time.

The blame game begins again.

You have been accused, as before, of blocking access to professionals.

You learn a new term,"gatekeeping".

And a new acronym, CIN, for Child in Need

How has this happened?

You have read numerous books and articles, desperate for ways to help your child.

You have attended webinars and searched for answers on a plethora of Facebook groups.

You have spent countless hours sitting with your child, in their sensory overwhelm, their panic and their despair.

Yet they are now considered a Child in Need due to concerns about your parenting.

The consultant doesn't believe you are to blame.

He tells you your child will engage when they are ready and able.

A lone voice, among a sea of others who say otherwise.

Some seeking to cover their own failures.

Some who are influenced by the louder voices.

Their views coloured by the fact these concerns have been raised before.

However groundless they were, and still are.

The consultant has faith in you, and you hope his experience and seniority will guide the others.

But even he bows to pressure when the word "safeguarding" is used.

As feared, questionable decisions are made.

Some barely ethical, but it appears when parents are blamed, priorities change.

You want, more than anything, to protect your child.

You know the proposals will cause your child to suffer. Unnecessarily.

Your inability to prevent this psychological harm to your child breaks your heart.

But any protestations simply fuel their belief you are preventing your child from engaging.

In this skewed world, you feel utterly powerless.

The familiar sense of dread returns.

You cannot prevent invasive thoughts from occupying your mind constantly.

Replaying conversations in your head.

How did you come across?

Were you believed?

Have you made things worse?

You imagine scenarios where you can calmly explain why the referral is not appropriate.

Where you are believed and vindicated.

This is a calm you are not able to feel in reality, as the mere sight of an email now sets your heart racing.

It is relentless, and exhausting, and all the while your child still needs you to be supporting them.

You are aware, of course, that your own anxiety must be impacting on your child.

However hard you try to hide it from them.

The professionals had this one right.

But how ironic that their interventions have caused this increased anxiety, that your child is now experiencing second hand.

You no longer view professionals as a source of guidance and support.

Your best hope is that they will not make your lives worse.

That this second merry-go-round of accusations, threats and lies will end soon.

Though the fear that it could happen yet again will linger.

You will not dare to ask for help.

To show vulnerability.

To describe how bad things have become.

The risk of unjustified blame is too great.

You wonder, when you have a moment to yourself, what if:

What if your voice had been heard from the start?

What if you had not been pressured to push your child into panic and fear, time and time again?

What if you had received support for your child and yourself, instead of blame?

What if your child had been offered the help they needed, anywhere along their heart-breaking journey into paralysing anxiety and despair?

What life might your child be living right now, had the professionals simply looked properly.

And realised that you weren't to blame?

Parental Blame and the Pathological Demand Avoidance Profile of Autism

In February 2023, Alice Running and Danielle Jata-Hall published a research report, "Parental Blame and the Pathological Demand Avoidance Profile of Autism". The research findings blew me away and confirmed what I had experienced and already knew: we have a culture of parent-blame that is hurting Neurodivergent families.

I have encountered hundreds of families of children who have a PDA Profile. It is estimated that 70% of children and young people with a PDA profile are not in school. Alice and Danielle's research shows that there is a culture of parent-blame towards parents and carers of PDA children in particular, but I believe it's pertinent for anyone raising Neurodivergent children.

With their permission, I am publishing an abridged version of their report findings here so that parents in Neurodivergent households might be better armed with up-to-date quantitative and qualitative data around the prevalence and impact of parent blame on families like their own.

Parental Blame and the Pathological Demand Avoidance Profile of Autism [abridged]
Alice Running and Danielle Jata-Hall, February 2023

"They blame me having therapy, not having therapy, being on medication, not being on medication, working, not working . . . they used to say I'm very cooperative, but as soon as I have refused to continue to use physical force to get my [Autistic] child in [to school], they [school professionals] reported me."

"There is no help just blame. I refuse to discuss my parenting further with professionals because it is viewed as my fault when in fact it works for my three children. I do what I have to, to keep everyone happy and safe. The less they know the better. Ultimately, I'm afraid of losing my children because the more you ask for help, the more they pick apart parenting, piling on the blame."

"It's hard to look for support and help and to feel you can open up and approach a professional when all you feel is judged and blamed and disbelieved . . ."

Introduction

Our research into parental blame and the PDA profile of autism was born from the personal experiences of the authors, who have both been subjected to misaligned scrutiny and blame by their respective local authorities in respect of their children's Autistic presentations.

This experience is not uncommon, with many families describing their experiences via social media groups on how they have been blamed for their Autistic children's presentation or perceived "lack of progress".

As a parent or carer, being blamed for some aspect of your child's disability by professionals working with your child is a frightening and isolating experience. Families with Autistic children fear losing their children to the care system, and the associated stigma around this fear can render sources of help as inaccessible.

Our survey – 'Parental Blame and the PDA Profile of Autism' – sought to understand the scope of this fear among parent / carers and establish how prevalent an issue parental blame is within the systems of support for Autistic / PDA children.

Alice Running (survey design, data analysis, report author)
www.alicerunningwriter.com

Alice Running writes about autism to create space for Autistic voices. She regularly writes about the Autistic experience, inclusivity and justice and has had articles published in *iNews*, *Metro*, *HuffPost*, *The Big Issue*, Yahoo, *SEN Magazine*, The Mighty and Special Needs Jungle. She also blogs at www.theautvocate.wordpress.com. Her book – *Helping Your Child with PDA Live a Happier Life* – is published by Jessica Kingsley Publishers. Alice is an Autistic woman, and mother to two Autistic children.

Danielle Jata-Hall (project development and survey dissemination)
www.pdaparenting.com

Danielle Jata-Hall is a parent of three Neurodivergent children and a blog writer at www.pdaparenting.com. She has worked in education supporting many children with SEND and has run a support group for other parents. She is a public speaker, PDA advocate and an online campaigner. With the support of her local MP, Danielle has succeeded in tabling an early day motion to get the PDA profile more nationally recognised.

She co-authored the children's book *I'm Not Upside Down, I'm Downside Up: Not a Boring Book About PDA* and is currently working on a fictional novel for adults called *Black Rainbow*.

What is the PDA (Pathological Demand Avoidance) profile of autism?

Pathological Demand Avoidance (PDA) is currently best understood as a distinct profile of autism, (O'Nions et al., 2016) with a key identifying characteristic being an anxiety-driven extreme avoidance of everyday demands, and a need for control which permeates all aspects of daily life.

Pathological Demand Avoidance (PDA) is not currently recognised within diagnostic manuals and there is some debate as to whether the label PDA is appropriate, as research hasn't yet shown it to be a discrete category within the Autistic spectrum (Green et al., 2018).

Recently developed practice guidance on the assessment and identification of a PDA profile of autism (PDA Society, 2022) explains that identification is necessary because it signposts the specific strategies that help, allowing personalisation and improved outcomes.

It is expected that many children and adults receive an autism diagnosis with a secondary identification of PDA or anxiety based / extreme demand avoidance, or similar terminology.

The recognition of Pathological Demand Avoidance (PDA) varies geographically, and whilst there are many professionals who understand the profile well, there remains a significant number of autism-related clinicians and professionals who either do not recognise the PDA profile or have too little an understanding of the profile.

This impacts the support families with an Autistic-PDA child receive and can lead to parent / carers finding themselves under safeguarding scrutiny.

For this study, we have collated information from families who consider their child to present as a child with the PDA profile of autism, whether they have diagnostic recognition of this or not.

What is "parental blame"?

Parental blame occurs when a relevant professional alleges or implies that a parent or carer is somehow causing their child's disability presentation.

For example, an Autistic child may no longer be thriving in a school environment and subsequently be unable to attend. Blame occurs when professionals intervene by suggesting that the non-attendance at school is caused by some form of parental failure.

Common forms of blame, in relation to autism and PDA, are:

Professionals stating that they do not observe the same Autistic presentations as parent / carers describe.

Professionals requesting that the parent / carer seek parental support in response to a disability need that an Autistic child is presenting with.

Professionals requesting that the parent / carer seek mental health support for themselves in response to a disability need that an Autistic child is presenting with.

Professionals alleging that an Autistic / PDA child's failure to progress against professional expectations is caused by some aspect of the parent / carer's personality, presentation or care for their child.

Professionals alleging that the parent / carer is inventing or exaggerating the needs of their Autistic / PDA child.

Professionals alleging that the parent / carer is somehow emotionally harming or neglecting their Autistic child, based on observations of the child's Autistic / PDA presentation.

Summary of Findings

Parents and carers of Autistic and / or PDA children can find themselves blamed for their children's disability presentations by professionals working with their families. Historically, this issue has been self-reported by individually affected families via parent-carer support groups and forums.

In 2022, our survey was conducted to ascertain the collective views of parent-carers of Autistic-PDA children, with a view to understanding:

- how prevalent professional blame towards parent-carers of Autistic-PDA children is,

- emerging patterns regarding the suscepti-
  bility of parent-carers to being blamed,

- how being blamed for their children's
  disability presentation feels for parent-
  carers, the impact of blame upon the
  family unit.

Data from 1016 parent-carer respondents
showed:

- 87.8% of parent-carer respondents said
  they had felt blamed for some aspect of
  their Autistic-PDA child's presentation or
  "lack of progress"
- 111 families (10.93% of respondents) had
  been subjected to some element of formal
  safeguarding procedures which cited the
  parent-carer at fault for the child's Autistic
  presentation
- of these 111 families subjected to formal
  safeguarding procedures, 57.66% were

237

headed by a lone mother and 76.57% were headed by a Neurodivergent parent.

- 68.46% of these families had a child with an accepted (NHS) diagnosis of autism.

Returned qualitative data demonstrates the devastating impact being exposed to blame can have on parent-carer wellbeing, family function and access to disability support.

Research Concluding Remarks

- **In situations where parent / carers are blamed for their Autistic / PDA child's presentation, it is the child that ultimately suffers.**
Families under scrutiny, due to allegations that they are responsible for their child's disability presentation, live with intense pressure, which can cause longer term difficulties within a family unit, such as trauma. When blame occurs, families

struggle to access the correct support for their child, either due to a fear of engaging with professionals, or because the type of support offered by professionals is not in line with an Autistic / PDA child's needs (and the advocating parent / carer is blamed, rather than seen as a source of expertise).

- **Systems of support for Autistic / PDA children can create mental health issues for the navigating parent / carer.**
Several respondents have talked about the creation of a self-fulfilling prophecy in relation to mental health – professionals have initially alleged that parent / carers have mental health needs, where there have been none, in explanation for a child's Autistic / PDA needs. This in turn has created distress, anxiety, and trauma for involved parents to an extent where

support for these emerging mental health needs has subsequently been required.

- **Certain types of parent / carers are more susceptible to the most extreme form of parental blame – safeguarding.**
Our findings show that safeguarding procedures are most prevalent amongst families headed by either a lone mother and / or Neurodivergent parent(s). Are professionals conflating adult Neurodivergent presentations with mental health concerns and / or parental obstruction? Are outdated stereotypes and assumptions surrounding Autistic people and lone mothers impacting decision making amongst professionals?

- **Neurodivergent parents are understandably fearful of disclosing their neurotype to supporting professionals.**
However, without disclosure parent / carers are unable to access reasonable adjustments

240

for themselves, which could improve communication with professionals and offer a certain level of legal protection against discriminative treatment.

- **There is a need for more autism / PDA informed professionals.**
  Increasing professional education around Neurodivergent parents could help minimise the misidentification of Neurodivergent presentations as safeguarding concerns. Increasing professional education around the PDA profile of autism could help minimise the misidentification of PDA parenting as permissive parenting.

You can access the unabridged research report, **Parental Blame and the Pathological Demand Avoidance Profile of Autism by Alice Running and Danielle Jata-Hall** on the resources section of the PDA Society Website at www.pdasociety.org.uk

House of Cards

By Charlotte Gale

Welcome to my house of cards,
Hypervigilance comes as standard
But the full panic attack
Will set you back
Somewhat.

It's not your average house,
Delicately, intricately constructed,
Bated breath,
With each card added
Adrenalin fuelled frenzy to hold it all
together when one card doesn't sit

Your Child is Not Broken

Quite
Right . . .

Lest it should all fall around you,

In a cataclysmic meltdown,

Coffee is on tap, and you'll convince
yourself that it's helping, fuelling your
resolve,
To hold together this fragile structure
Really though, you know,
It just makes your heart race,
As you try to keep everything in place

The cards are not of Jokers,
Kings and Queens
But husbands,
Dogs,
And quirky teens.
Neurodivergent needs

That overlap or clash
And the breeze of uncertainty that
murmurs constant threat

Yet,

For the most part
My house of cards stands tall.

And on the days where all is well,
The "good" days, of smiles,
Successes, and harmony
The sun streams through the cracks
Lighting up the house of cards in all its
Iridescent fragility,
Luminescent beauty.

And you allow yourself to become lost
In a moment of gratitude,
Reflecting upon how far these cards have
come.

Your Child is Not Broken

No longer crumpled and bent out of shape
by the rough handling of others
But tall,
Wearing the lines as battle scars,
As an ode to their strength,

You take your eye off the ball

Or rather, a wall.

It only takes one.
A moment of self-indulgent reminiscing
To bring a shift in balance.
A need not met,

An overload,
Intrusive thoughts,
It all smells wrong!

And in the blink of an eye,
And as though it happens to some dramatic
song,
The House of cards collapses.

Again.

Like putting out fires, you'll find the
source
Among the debris of angst and tears,
Or the dis-regulated yelling
As the others shield their ears.

The cards have fallen.

You ignore the voice,
The whispers of self-judgement,
That would chastise and reprimand.
Not today.
You're needed.

Your Child is Not Broken

So, you drown them in more coffee,
As you roll up your sleeves
And pick up the cards

One
By
One.

You lovingly smooth them,

Uncrumple their edges
And stand them up,
With all the help they need,
Taking heed

They could fall again at any time.

Which is why,
Although risky
And self-indulgent,

Basking in the moments of perfect balance
is vital.

However fragile
However transient or fleeting,

Those are the moments that fuel you,
That warm you,

As once again you re-build your House of
Cards.

And Finally . . .

After the book was first published in the early part of 2023, I received hundreds of emails from parents and carers, sharing their own experiences with me. Some folks told me about their "touch the gate" adventures, or variations thereof.

I went to my online community and, together, we compiled another list of fuckery said to parents in Neurodivergent households. I asked my community to tell me "What ridiculous things have been said to you? What stupid suggestions have been made? What 'advice' has made your hair curl?" and I compiled a list of the most-common and most ridiculous, from over 400 responses.

With that list, I made you a Bullshit Bingo card. Use it however you see fit. Take it to meetings so you can tick off the phrases in real-time, to remind yourself that you are not alone.

Grab yourself a bingo dabber.

Eyes down for a Line of Lame Shit and a Full House of Fuckery . . .

Your Child is Not Broken

BULLSHIT BINGO

"He doesn't look Autistic"	"And how are YOU, Mum?"	"You need to set firm boundaries"	"What's going on at home?"	"Have you tried taking away all devices?"
"In the real world . . ."	"I have been a teacher for 25 years . . ."	"Resilience!"	"They are fine in school"	"We all have to do things we don't like"
"We didn't have all this autism in our day"	"We don't recognise PDA"	"Safe-guarding!"	"Have you considered home educating?"	"They need to make better choices"
"You won't get an EHCP"	"We can't be seen to be giving anyone preferential treatment"	"Mum says . . ."	"Have you tried a reward chart?"	"They know exactly what they are doing"
"Why do you want to label your child"	"If they won't engage, we'll have to discharge you"	"Everyone masks – it's a positive coping strategy"	"Eye contact!"	"They are picking up on your anxiety"

References

Some of the research referred to in the book has been excluded from this list intentionally, because it was funded by organisations or linked to researchers who take a pathologised view of neurodivergence. In those instances, the source is referenced in the main body of the book so that readers can find the original research if they wish.

- Attendance and Prosecution Thresholds Data, 2021/2022, ffteducationdatalab.org.uk

- 'A Conceptual Analysis of Autistic Masking: Understanding the Narrative of Stigma and the Illusion of Choice', *Autism in Adulthood* vol. 3 no. 1, Amy Pearson and Kieran Rose, 2021

- Institutionalising Parent-carer Blame, cerebra.org.uk, 2021.

- *Medical News Today* Ableism Definition, medicalnewstoday.com

- 'Pervasiveness and correlates of implicit attitudes and Stereotypes', Brian A. Nosek et al, *European Review of Psychology*, 2007.

- 'Racial/Ethnic Disparities in the Identification of Children With Autism Spectrum Disorders' – David S Mandell, et al, *American Journal of Public Health*, March 2009.

- SEND Attendance Data, Office of National Statistics, October 2022

- Special Education Needs Data for Academic Year 2021/2022, Office of National Statistics, 2022

- Dr Stephen Porges, Polyvagal Theory website, stephenporges.com

- 'What Is the Male-to-Female Ratio in Autism Spectrum Disorder? A Systematic Review and Meta-Analysis', Rachel Loomes, Laura Hull, William Polmear Locke Mandy, *Journal of the American Academy of Child and Adolescent Psychiatry*, June 2017

- 'Parental Blame and the Pathological Demand Avoidance Profile of Autism', Alice Running and Danielle Jata-Hall, February 2023, pda.org.uk

Helpful Links and Resources

This is not intended as an exhaustive list, but it's a signpost to places I think you may find helpful. For up-to-date resources and signposting, visit my website at www.heidimavir.com

Autistic and Neurodivergent Identity
Autistic, Typing
www.facebook.com/AutisticTyping/

Fidgets and Fries
www.instagram.com/fidgets.and.fries/

Jude Afolake Olubodun
www.instagram.com/theemidnightgospel/

Kristy Forbes
www.kristyforbes.com.au

Kieran Rose
www.theautisticadvocate.com

Neuroclastic
www.neuroclastic.com

Neurodivergent Rebel
www.neurodivergentrebel.com

PDA
Missing the Mark
www.missingthemark.blog

PDA Parenting
www.pdaparenting.com

PDA Society

www.pdasociety.org.uk

EHCP Help and Support

EOTAS Matters

www.facebook.com/seNDSupport

IPSEA

www.ipsea.org.uk

Send Family Instincts

www.sendfamilyinstincts.com

Barriers to Attendance

Not Fine In School

www.notfineinschool.co.uk

Square Peg

www.teamsquarepeg.org

Mental Health Support

Association of Neurodivergent Therapists

www.neurodivergenttherapists.com

Confidential support for children and young
people

Childline

0800 1111

Prevention of young suicide

Papyrus

www.papyrus-uk.org

The Samaritans

116 123

Shout

www.giveusashout.org

or text 85358

Young Minds
www.youngminds.org.uk

Targeted Support

ADHD UK
www.adhduk.co.uk/

British Dyslexia Association
www.bdadyslexia.org.uk

For those experiencing eating disorders
Beat
www.beateatingdisorders.org.uk

For families of children with brain conditions
Cerebra
www.cerebra.org.uk

Council for Disabled Children
www.councilfordisabledchildren.org.uk

Dyspraxia Foundation

www.dyspraxiafoundation.org.uk

Ehlers-Danlos Society

www.ehlers-danlos.com

For gender non-conforming folks

Gendered Intelligence

www.genderedintelligence.co.uk

Support and advice for young people up to 25

The Mix

www.themix.org.uk

For trans kids and their families

Mermaids

www.mermaidsuk.org.uk

Help, advice and support around PANS and
PANDAS

PANS PANDAS UK

www.panspandasuk.org

For LGBTQIA+ youth

The Proud Trust

www.theproudtrust.org

Child to Parent Abuse

PEGS

www.pegsupport.co.uk

Cerebral Palsy

Scope

www.cerebralpalsy.org.uk

Tourettes Action

www.tourettes-action.org.uk

Acknowledgements

This book would not exist were it not for the help and support of some incredible humans. Specifically,

I am forever grateful to:

Christopher Lushypants Excellent Teeth
Cathy Beveridge
Lydia Bernsmeier-Rullow
Beth Bodycote
Jess Cain
Kirsteen Chassels
Ellie Costello

Steph Curtis

Eleanor Dyde

Tom Fadden

Naomi Fisher

Kristy Forbes

Eliza Fricker

Danielle Jata-Hall

Jodie Hammersley

Holly Hodgson-Simmons

Kate Jones

Laura Kerbey

Olivia Kessel

Amber Lane

Susan Liverman

Jo McMeechan

Isabel Rees

Paula Rice

Kim Roberts

Maddie Roberts

Carol Robinson

Kieran Rose

El Rumsby

Alice Running

Anna Sackley

Karen Stepanova

Terra Vance

Theo Waddington

Lyn Wall

Katie West

The Unstoppable Parents and the EOTAS
Matters Community